Praise for *Everything I Need to Know About Being a Manager,*
I Learned from my Kids

'It seems like a stroke of genius for Ian Durston to relate
management behaviours and values to those of parenthood.
I am sure all readers of his book will find it of enormous help
in both their professional and personal lives.'
Iain Gray, Managing Director and General Manager,
Airbus UK (and father of four)

'This is an excellent book, not just funn~
full of strategic insights f~
to improve their relatic
at home or in the workp.
Peter Hyman, former F
Strategic Communicatio

'An excellent read. Ian Dursto~ ~ccumulated a lot
of insight and perspective from a~ ~at he has been exposed to
throughout his career and home life. As a proud father
of 16-year-old quadruplets and the proud leader of a thriving
consultancy, with all the responsibilities, challenges and
fulfilment that comes with both, I related to all that he wrote.'
David Owen, Managing Director,
UK Consulting, Deloitte

'An original and worthwhile book on management
is hard to find nowadays, but this is one.'
Tim O'Connor, Director of N.T.S. Ltd. (and father of two)

'The humorous blend of anecdote and theory
make this book both enjoyable and accessible.'
Dr Phil Jones, Lecturer in Management,
University of Leicester (and father of one)

'Very enjoyable and very accessible ... I found myself laughing
out loud at some points and smirking knowingly at others.'
Rosemary Dyson, Consultant

'This book demonstrates the clear link between management and
parenthood and is a must read for managers and parents alike.'
Jeff Jackson, 9.9 World Class Performance Ltd,
Team Specialist and Personal Coach (and father of three)

Ian Durston has worked in industry and business for 14 years, including
a role at Deloitte Consulting, where his clients included Vodafone,
Barclays Bank, General Motors and the Ministry of Defence. He is
currently a senior project manager at Airbus. He lives with his wife and
three sons near Bristol. This is his first book.

Everything I Need to Know about Being a Manager, I Learned From my Kids

IAN DURSTON

piatkus

To contact Ian Durstan, visit www.beyond-online.co.uk

PIATKUS

First published in Great Britain in 2007 by Piatkus Books Ltd
This paperback edition published in 2009 by Piatkus

Page 143: Extract from *Toddler Taming* (revised and updated) by
Dr Christopher Green.
Published in 2006. Reprinted by permission of Random House Australia.

A CIP catalogue record for this book
is available from the British Library

ISBN 978-0-7499-4224-3

Edited by Andy Armitage
Text design by Tara O'Leary
Typeset by Action Publishing Technology
Printed and bound in Great Britain by
Clays Ltd, St Ives plc

Papers used by Piatkus are natural, renewable and recyclable
products sourced from well-managed forests and certified
in accordance with the rules of the Forest Stewardship Council.

Mixed Sources
Product group from well-managed
forests and other controlled sources
www.fsc.org Cert no. SGS-COC-004081
© 1996 Forest Stewardship Council

Piatkus
An imprint of
Little, Brown Book Group
100 Victoria Embankment
London EC4Y 0DY

An Hachette UK Company
www.hachette.co.uk

www.piatkus.co.uk

For Melanie, Jack, Sam and Will.

If –

If you can keep your head when all about you
      Are losing theirs and blaming it on you,
If you can trust yourself when all men doubt you,
      But make allowance for their doubting too;
If you can wait and not be tired by waiting,
      Or being lied about, don't deal in lies,
Or being hated, don't give way to hating,
      And yet don't look too good, nor talk too wise:

If you can dream – and not make dreams your master;
      If you can think – and not make thoughts your aim;
If you can meet Triumph and Disaster
      And treat those two impostors just the same;
If you can bear to hear the truth you've spoken
      Twisted by knaves to make a trap for fools,
Or watch the things you gave your life to, broken,
      And stoop and build 'em up with worn-out tools:

If you can make one heap of all your winnings
      And risk it on one turn of pitch-and-toss,
And lose, and start again at your beginnings
      And never breathe a word about your loss;
If you can force your heart and nerve and sinew
      To serve your turn long after they are gone,
And so hold on when there is nothing in you
      Except the will which says to them: 'Hold on!'

If you can talk with crowds and keep your virtue,
      Or walk with kings – nor lose the common touch,
If neither foes nor loving friends can hurt you,
      If all men count with you, but none too much;
If you can fill the unforgiving minute
      With sixty seconds' worth of distance run,
Yours is the Earth and everything that's in it,
      And – which is more – you'll be a Man, my son!

Rudyard Kipling

Contents

Introduction

Becoming a Parent

'It is frightening when we realise our parents aren't perfect.'

The Hood, *Thunderbirds* (2004)

'I JUST want to be in Stafford!' my wife screamed.

I glanced up from the vicelike headlock that Melanie had me in at the time and the midwife peered round from between her knees. The midwife and I exchanged puzzled looks. We knew childbirth was painful, and I'm sure she had heard many a terrifying yelp of agony over the years, but surely this must be pain in the extreme. Stafford?

The contraction continued for what seemed like for ever (being in increasingly tighter and tighter headlocks for 12 hours isn't easy, you know) until it finally subsided to allow Melanie a chance to get ready for the next one. Oh, what fun! It was the middle of the night in Southmead hospital, Bristol. Our previous evening in front of the telly watching *The Kumars at No. 42* (it's worrying that such an absurd TV programme will now be for ever etched on my memory) had been rudely interrupted by the onset of labour.

During the few minutes of relative normality between the contractions, the midwife and I were granted an explanation for the aforementioned outburst. Stafford, or at least the M6 running past Stafford, was where Melanie's parents were probably now located. Having received the preplanned phone call the evening before, they were now on their journey from the northwest down to Bristol to help out once their grandchild had been delivered into this world. Apparently, it was therefore logical that Stafford would be a perfectly understandable place to want to be. Worrying.

No sooner had we got the Stafford situation sorted out than the next contraction started and the midwife and I were back to our positions, she crouching as if about to receive the ball from the back of a rugby scrum and I back in the headlock looking like Marvin the Meathead from Saturday-afternoon wrestling in the days when *World of Sport* was cool (or was that just me?).

It was while adopting this position, with Melanie's fingers rammed up one nostril and poking in both eyes, that I recalled the antenatal class we had both attended sometime earlier. Topic of the week: 'The Birth'. A young midwife had sat calmly on a chair in front of a small circle of bemused and naïve parents-to-be. She took a battered old doll in one hand and her home-knitted cardigan in the other. She then, face completely deadpan, proceeded to push the doll through the sleeve of the cardigan, head first, until it gently and quietly emerged from the cuff end. This was done while she uttered something about birth canal and breathing deeply, followed by, 'Of course, it's not quite as easy as that in reality.' I couldn't agree more. Quite frankly, an evening watching Tiny Tears being shoved down an old cardy, while sipping weak tea, was no preparation whatsoever for what I was currently going through. Melanie wasn't finding it easy, either!

The contractions came and went for most of the rest of the night until finally, at 11.25 the following morning, Samuel David Durston shot into this world. I have never been so relieved – although I do have to admit feeling slight concern at the time over whether or not my previously rather nice white T-shirt would ever find its original shape and colour again.

Within the hour, Sam and I were enjoying our first football match together. It was World Cup 2002 time and some obscure game between two unheard-of countries, both of whom had probably beaten the French, was on the TV. Sam 'watched' a bit but then got bored and nodded off to sleep in my arms. What a life, I thought: an hour old and he's spent 10 minutes in the bath, 20 minutes watching the footy and half an hour asleep – what bliss. Our second child had arrived.

Our first child, Jack Arthur, had been born in the John Radcliffe hospital in Oxford roughly two years earlier – an altogether different experience. A few weeks before his due date, while cosily curled up in the womb, Jack showed the first signs of what has since become a bad habit – a tendency to be stubborn. Having spent eight and a half months cooperating in what was a straightforward pregnancy, now that his grand arrival was fast approaching he decided that he would rather be the other way up. He thus promptly turned round to get himself into a convenient breach position – that is, gangly, dangly, pointing in odd directions legs first rather than smooth, round, conveniently shaped head first. Great. We spent the next few weeks playing Travis's song 'Turn' loudly on the stereo, but to no avail. The little poppet was having none of it.

After weighing up all the options, we decided that the best thing for us to do was to have an elective caesarean delivery. It seemed the safest approach for both mother and baby. So, on a sunny August morning, we drove from our home to the hospital for our 'appointment'. It was bizarre, really, since all the preparations over the previous months had been for something quite different. Psychologically I was gearing myself up for waters breaking in the middle of Marks & Spencer, a mad drive across town, honking the horn in dense traffic, wife lying on back seat screaming 'It's coming!' and arriving at the hospital in the nick of time for perfect baby to be delivered by Dr Kildare, assisted by plenty of hot soapy water and clean towels.

But no. Instead, the alarm clock had gone off at a perfectly reasonable 8.30 am. We had gone through all the normal morning routines involving bathrooms and breakfast as on any other day. The drive to the hospital had all been done under the speed limit while we listened to Radio 4. We had stopped off at the newsagent to buy a paper to remind us of the day (long since disappeared) and spent some time driving round the hospital car park looking for a 'strategic' spot at optimum distance from both the entrance and the pay-and-display machine.

When we walked into the building we were shown to a small empty waiting room and told to make ourselves comfortable and a doctor would be along to see us within an hour. Melanie put down our bag of spare clothes, nappies and Babygros while I sorted us out with coffee. Not long after, another couple arrived, with bag, and sat themselves down, and then a third couple joined us a few minutes later.

There we were, three heavily pregnant women, three bags and three twitchy blokes, all exchanging polite chitchat. We might as well have been in a waiting room at the hairdresser or dentist, or waiting for the car to finish having its new exhaust fitted. Instead we were all there to experience the greatest miracle of life – at our respective, allotted times. I gazed around at the three bumps thinking how strange it was that in a few hours' time three little 'bundles of fun' would have joined us.

After a morning of waiting in this bizarre situation, Melanie was finally taken off to be prepared for the 'operation' and I was shown to a room and given a rather fetching set of theatre clothes in which to kit myself out. I was then taken to the delivery room, where Melanie was already waiting.

I have to admit that I had been dreading this moment almost all my life. To describe me as squeamish is a bit of an understatement. I start to feel a bit strange when people get things in their eye and I can't bear to look at the rucked-up elbow skin when people straighten their arms. Weird, I admit. One of the biggest disasters in my life was being told that my final-year project at university was titled 'Robotics in Brain Surgery' and having to go and watch a live brain operation the day after a particularly good party the night before. Not one of my moments of glory, as my project partner will testify.

My fear had always been that, no matter what the type of birth, the arrival of my first child stood a good chance of coinciding with my lying flat out on the delivery room floor with some overweight midwife scoffing and muttering something about men being good for next to nothing. The fact that we were having a caesarean and the room that I was walking into looked like something out of a particularly unpleasant episode of *ER* was not exactly helping matters.

For those who have not experienced a caesarean, the doctors are at least reasonably understanding and erect a drape across your partner's chest so, if you don't want to, you don't have to observe the details of what's going on. I therefore elected to sit on a stool next to Melanie's head and cowered behind this screen making sure I didn't accidentally get a glimpse of anything unpleasant. As I held Melanie's hand, it wasn't completely clear who was supporting whom. When things got started, a friendly nurse stood next to me eagerly looking over the screen to watch all that was going on while turning to me at regular intervals to say, 'Are you sure you don't want to watch?' I could have strangled her.

After about five or ten minutes of activity on the other side of the screen, one of the two doctors suddenly lifted a small, wet, pink bundle of arms and legs into the air. I think his precise words were 'There you go' – as if he were delivering some package from UPS. It was all a bit surreal – having not been brave enough to look over the screen, for all I knew he could have just taken this baby out of a set of drawers underneath the bed. But Jack Arthur had arrived. What's more, I was still conscious. Result.

While Melanie was being sewn up, a nurse checked all Jack's fingers and toes. She even got me to agree with her that they were all there, as if, should any be found to be missing later, it would all be my fault! The responsibilities of fatherhood had started already. After Melanie and Jack had been sorted out, they were both wheeled down the corridor to a nearby ward, with me following and looking proud. When we got to the ward the other two mothers from the waiting room were already there. I shook the fathers' hands.

A nurse then came up to me, thrust a Babygro from our bag into my hands and said, 'There you go, pop him in that, will you?' You might as well have asked me to give a nuclear submarine an annual service. Nobody had told me that I would be expected to carry out a task of such complexity no more than half an hour after the birth. For goodness' sake, I had just got through the whole thing without fainting, hadn't I? Was that not enough? I fumbled around with my new son for the next 15 minutes and eventually managed to get him into the Babygro without breaking anything and even getting his legs and arms in the right bits. I'm sure the nurse was looking at Jack and wondering what he had done in a previous life to deserve a father like this in this one.

By the time our third child, William Henry, came along, things seemed almost routine – apart, that is, from a three-mile drive down the hard shoulder of the M5 in order to avoid an early-morning rush-hour jam, while Melanie puffed and panted in the passenger seat coping with the early stages of labour. With Will's arrival, our family was complete.

However, the subsequent process of raising our children has been far from routine and has made their births seem straightforward in comparison. I will never forget how difficult things were after Jack was born and we tried to cope with the arrival of our first child: a feed every few hours that didn't go well; being woken every two hours at night; changing his nappy every five minutes; cooking meals; doing the washing; sterilising bottles; finding time to go shopping.

During the two weeks of paternity leave that I took after the birth, I remember frantically tidying the house and kitchen the whole time in some desperate and vain attempt to feel in control. We weren't. Every day it would get to about 2 pm and both of us would still be in our dressing gowns (Melanie and I, that is) looking dreadful, feeling dreadful and wondering when we were going to get time to have a shower and put some clothes on. I was always very conscious that in only a few days' time I would have to go back to work, at which point getting dressed at two in the afternoon was going to prove more of a problem.

At no point in our few years on this planet does life change so suddenly and drastically. When you come out of that hospital carrying the little bundle of loveliness, your life has changed beyond recognition. The rewards, of course, are immeasurable, but the investment is considerable too.

Becoming a Manager

'Being in charge was hard work!'

Scoop, *Bob the Builder*

BECOMING a parent is difficult. Becoming a manager, while a touch less emotional than becoming a mum or dad, is no breeze, either.

As with becoming a parent, being made a manger usually involves being thrown in at the deep end. The hours will probably be long and the responsibilities somewhat daunting. All of a sudden all the people who were your mates aren't sure if they should trust you any more and the people you went to for help expect you to sort the problems out by yourself now. Often the person who knows most about the position you're filling has kindly disappeared to some other company or retired in Eastbourne, leaving only a good luck note and a few bits of tatty stationery in the bottom of their old desk drawer. Being a manager is difficult.

I know. I'm a manager myself. I work for the UK arm of Airbus, managing a team designing and building wings. I love my job – it's an amazing buzz taking a team of people on a journey from a blank piece of paper to seeing a completed aeroplane flying overhead. However, it's not an easy journey. The stress levels are high – when deadlines are approaching, they're *very* high. The technology is complex, but has to be 100 per cent safe. The right people are difficult to recruit, so team members are stretched and under a lot of pressure. Budgets are tight. There are all sorts of different people from different suppliers, countries and cultures to coordinate. The challenges are numerous.

As part of my job, I sometimes have to fly to Toulouse in southwest France, where the wings are assembled onto the rest of the aircraft. On one flight, having settled into my seat, I was handed a copy of the *Daily Telegraph* with which to pass the two-hour journey. As I browsed through the usual pages reporting war, drought, famine and pestilence (and that was just East Anglia), an article caught my eye with the following headline: *Struggling Middle Managers Put Companies in Jeopardy.*

The article informed me that middle managers are under such severe strain that the future success of many companies is at real risk. Oh, dear! I thought. The article continued to talk about the long hours that managers worked, the amount of sleep they lost worrying about problems, the lack of training, the pressure, the burden of responsibility, the missed family commitments, the stress … Oh, dear, oh, dear! I thought. I could relate to it all.

As I read through this cheery news, I thought back to the start of my own career. I was not long out of university when I was first asked to lead a small team of people carrying out a product-development programme. I was working in an automotive-components factory in Birmingham, just north of Spaghetti Junction. (The friends I graduated with were very envious, since they had to struggle with jobs in the media, banking and marketing down in boring London!) I was very keen and enthusiastic, but also very green.

One of my first tasks in charge was to get some parts made on the shop floor in order to be sent off to the company's research-and-development centre for testing. I promptly organised an appropriate slot on the appropriate machine and arranged for one member of my team to supply all the appropriate drawings to the appropriate operator – all on schedule. I was starting to think this management lark was pretty straightforward. The parts were then made – on the night shift. The guy from R&D rang up to find out when he could have them. As they needed to be measured before I supplied them to him, I told him, somewhat smugly, that he could have them the next day after they had all been through the inspection centre. The next day I came into work looking forward to delivering the parts and ticking off the first completed task on the team's project plan. My own boss *was* going to be pleased.

I have since learned that the night shift is not always the best shift on which to get something new done. During the process of measuring all the parts it turned out that every single one of them was completely out of spec. Here I was, trying to develop an improved product, and all I had was a crate full of scrap. I had to ring up the guy from R&D and tell him the parts were useless and he was going to have to wait at least two weeks before he got some more.

I also had to explain to my boss why I had just spent £5,000 on a crate of parts that were no use whatsoever on any type of car and would fetch only a few quid from the local scrap-metal merchant. I was mortified. These days, when you're building wings, £5,000 isn't much, but back then it was more than the student overdraft I had just spent the last two years trying to pay off. I had made my managerial debut, but was wondering whether it might just be better to ask if I could go back to being told what to do and letting somebody else take all the responsibility.

A few years later, when I worked as a management consultant, I found that I wasn't the only one finding management difficult – there were plenty of other people, across all sectors of business and industry, who were facing similar problems.

As the plane approached the Toulouse runway, my mind wandered back to the present. I realised there was no doubt about it, the *Daily Telegraph* was right: there are struggling middle managers everywhere. I ripped out the article and put it in my bag. 'Need to think about this,' I said to myself. I also thought how interesting it was that the challenges I face as a manager now are pretty much the same as I had faced as a spotty graduate several years earlier. Some of the numbers are now bigger, but the things to worry about haven't changed – losing sleep, being required to work long hours, keeping team members happy, time away from family, lack of training, stress, frustration ...

The question was, how did I make sure that I didn't end up a struggling middle manager myself?

The Connection

'I can do one of two things: I can be President of the United States or I can control my daughter. I cannot possibly do both.'

Theodore (Teddy) Roosevelt, 26th President of the USA

THE remarkable thing, both about becoming a parent and becoming a manager, is that anybody can do it. Actually, what I really mean is that anybody is *allowed* to do it. In the days when you needed a dog licence, I would have been a rich man if I had a pound for every time I read in the press about some family breakdown and the fact that it was harder to get a licence for a dog than to bring a child into this world. Well, it's the same with management.

In this country, at least we require teachers and doctors, for example, to have varying levels of qualifications before they are allowed to lift a piece of chalk or a stethoscope in anger. When it comes to management, though, anybody is allowed to have a go. In fact, it's worse than that: most of us are made managers because we were good at something else! It's the accountant who always balances the books, or the software programmer who writes the best code who gets to be boss of all the other accountants or programmers. Yes, people are promoted because they are recognised as being very capable, but capable of something else, not necessarily management.

What skills do you need to be a good manager, then? Well, if you ever ask a group of workers to compile a list of things that describe a good manager, they will usually come up with something along the following lines:

- sets clear objectives
- is friendly and approachable
- has a good sense of humour
- is good at listening
- is focused
- is inspirational.

You will realise fairly quickly by looking through the list that it is all to do with soft, people-type characteristics. Technical capabilities do sometimes get mentioned but they are often towards the bottom of the list. I have seen this exercise carried out twice, once with a bunch of management consultants in expensive suits and once with a bunch of engineers in not so expensive suits. The results were incredibly similar, and the conclusion was clear: management is all about people. That parenting is all about people, albeit little ones, can hardly be disputed.

During the course of bringing up my children, and the nine-to-five routine of life as a manager, this connection between parenting and management has become more and more apparent to me. It's slowly dawned on me that the answer to my question at the end of the flight to Toulouse has been right under my nose – the kids. There's so much that I do at home with the children that I can apply in the office. One minute I'm negotiating with three young boys over what time they have to go to bed, the next I'm negotiating with a supplier over a contract price. As I've travelled between work and home, it's amazed me how many parallels can be drawn and how much of what I've had to learn in order to cope with the challenges of being a parent is actually also really useful when I'm coping with the challenges of being a manager.

I've realised that this means two things. First, since parenting and management processes are so similar (both are all about people), there are methods and techniques that can be used for both. Second, by understanding some of the characteristics of children that stay with them for life, you can better understand the adults that you are managing today and at least attempt to understand what makes them tick. Don't get me wrong: as a manger you can't copy what you do as a parent. But you can definitely learn from it.

This book, therefore, is a collection of everything I've learned from my own parenting experiences that has also helped me improve as a manager. I hope that it will help you improve as a manager too. It is about people and how to manage them. It is about how to have that certain something that sets you apart from the group and makes you a manager, the soft, fuzzy stuff that comes down to your style as an individual and how you use yourself, your charisma and personality to influence people and persuade them that they want to work towards the common objective.

A boss of mine summed it up perfectly when we were discussing my yearly appraisal and my own behaviours. 'Ian,' he said thoughtfully, 'being a good manager is all about developing the Ready Brek glow.' I pondered on the image of myself walking about with an orange shimmer around me. Could be interesting. He continued, 'When you're in a meeting, looking at some problem, people have got to be glad that you're there. They've got to feel that, with you there, they've got the best chance of getting the problem sorted.'

When I was first made a manager, I really struggled with what I needed to do that was different from the time before I was a manager. I knew I wasn't suddenly going to be setting corporate strategy and I could do all the stuff on Gantt charts and so on with my eyes shut. I knew that there was something else in between that I needed to learn about and do differently – the Ready Brek glow. Hopefully, after reading this book, you will be able to develop an orange shimmer of your own!

LEADERSHIP

'Leadership is not magnetic personality – that can just as well be a glib tongue. It is not "making friends and influencing people" – that is flattery. Leadership is lifting a person's vision to higher sights, the raising of a person's performance to a higher standard, the building of a personality beyond its normal limitations.'

Peter F. Drucker, management guru

BEING a good leader and providing strong leadership is a critical part of being a good manager. Not that other areas aren't important, but leadership stands out as essential. It's not a 'nice-to-have' – without it you might as well forget management.

Everybody can name some great leaders: Winston Churchill, John F. Kennedy, Montgomery, Richard Branson, Elizabeth I, Scott of the Antarctic, Bob Paisley (OK, maybe not up there with Churchill, but Liverpool were a great football team in the seventies). But defining what makes a great leader (or let's settle for good, even) is a much harder task. Something about charisma usually gets touted about, but it's much more complicated then that.

Forgetting world politics, and Anfield greats, leadership in terms of management means two things:

- Giving your team direction – setting the strategy

- Having the personality and characteristics to take them with you

It's much the same as a parent. OK, when it comes to setting a strategy, you may not assemble your kids together at the beginning of the year and say, 'Right, this year we are going to increase turnover by 20 per cent by expanding into European markets while working our fixed assets harder, and this is how we're going to do it.' But when that little bundle of fun arrives, if not before, every parent has got some sort of direction for them mapped out. Go on – admit it.

Aged 1   Walking, talking, eating solids.

Aged 5   Reading Shakespeare, writing novels, swimming like a fish.

Aged 10   All-round academic and sportsperson, popular at school, starting to compose short symphonies.

Aged 16   Ten GCSEs at grade A, running own part-time business, popular with the opposite sex.

Aged 18   Numerous A levels.

Aged 21   Graduating from Cambridge in brain surgery, partner to die for.

And, when it comes to ensuring they follow that direction, you don't sit down with the kids in their early years and say, 'OK, that's the plan, off you go and get back to me when the surgery in Harley Street is raking in the cash to top up my pension.' There does tend to be a certain amount of coaxing, cajoling and guiding along the way. Parents are constantly summoning up as much character as possible to try to take the kids on that journey successfully.

Now I know what you're saying: 'But I'm not one of those pushy types that appear on TV documentaries about mad parents – as long as my child is happy, I'm happy, it doesn't matter what they achieve.' And I would totally agree – I have (and I hope will continue to have) a very similar philosophy myself. But that in itself is a direction – it's a strategy. There are all sorts of strategies – bringing up our kids up in an atmosphere of fun, taking them to church every Sunday, encouraging them to play with a mix of different children – all with the aim of developing our children into the types of adults that we aspire for them to be and giving them a direction to grow in.

And, generally, a parent spends a minimum of 16 years taking each child on that journey. En route, at every stage, parents are tested to the full in order to keep their kids on the track that they want for them. And sometimes the kids even end up something like the young adult who was hoped for.

Have a Strategy

'To Infinity and beyond!'

Buzz Lightyear, *Toy Story* (1995)

WITH regard to leadership, I'm very reluctant to use the term *strategy*, since it tends to conjure up images of all-knowing, highly paid chief executives dealing with highbrow concepts. In this context, though, this isn't what I mean by strategy. I use the word in its broadest sense to mean anything that is giving a team of people, no matter how small or large, a direction to go in. It can be a short-term direction, or more long-term. Whatever the level, though, strategy is the reason why you are leading.

When it comes to setting your own strategy, in my experience, the more simple and straightforward you can make things the better. People's working days are full of detail, clutter, nitty-gritty and complications. They don't want to have to digest and commit to memory some in-depth analysis, calculations and conclusions to understand where you are taking them and why.

A recent TV advert comes to mind of an executive collecting his team together and dropping several copies of a weighty management consultancy report on the table and asking the room of unimpressed faces to digest it and come back with how they're going to implement it. It just doesn't work. Writing in the *Sunday Times*, Brian Appleyard tells how Richard Branson always asks for things to be put in the simplest terms, partly because he's dyslexic, but, more importantly, because any strategy that is strong and simple has far more impact in his busy world. If it's good enough for Sir Richard, it's good enough for me.

Also, your strategy doesn't necessarily have to be anything formal, but it should be something you have thought about and communicated clearly to your team (in some form or another). People need to understand what the big picture is, where you're taking them and where they fit in. They need to know why you are there. If you don't have a strategy, a *raison d'être*, and all you intend to do is maintain the status quo, or let people decide for themselves what needs to be done, then why bother?

If you've ever played a musical instrument, you will probably know that, given a piece of music that everyone is familiar with, an orchestra can usually get by with a bad conductor or without one at all. A good conductor, though, puts his or her own mark on the music and brings it to life and makes it something different and special. Similarly, people can, and often do, get by with bad managers. A good manager, though, armed with a well-communicated strategy – a clear idea of what he or she wants people to do – can achieve something special.

A word of caution here. When you arrive in your new management position, take some time to learn about the role, the people and the challenges before you decide on what your strategy is and thrust it upon your workforce. For many, the temptation to announce their arrival with a range of new initiatives is irresistible and seen as something that must be done to show their strong leadership right from the beginning. It's assumed that whatever was done previously must be wrong and that change is imperative. This may be the case – but make sure you're right first.

Doing something new is not an insignificant undertaking. I have had a lot more respect for managers who have started a new role and done very little different for the first few months and spent the time getting to know the people and understanding the issues. When they do then start to make their mark on the job, their approach and strategy is invariably a much better one than that of somebody who has arrived with all guns blazing. They've done their homework and they've got buy-in. The trick here is to judge the timing right. Holding back for too long makes you look like the bad conductor, but jumping in feet first can just make you look silly. It's all down to your judgement.

Don't Change the Strategy ...

'If you fear making anyone mad, then you ultimately probe for the lowest common denominator of human achievement.'

Jimmy Carter, 39th President of the USA

ONE of the things you quickly learn when you're a manager is that the occasions are rare when everybody is in agreement with what you are doing and will all rally round to follow your direction and sing your praises. In fact, these occasions are in the region of zero. Leaders just don't please everybody, and they spend a lot of time getting people to do things they don't really want to do. If you cave in on what you want to do because one person isn't in agreement, or because you come up against resistance generally, then you'll never get anywhere or achieve anything.

It's exactly the same with children. The number of times that my three want to watch the same video or go to the same park are limited. In fact, I know they take great joy in disagreeing on purpose. (There's obviously some gene there that gives them great satisfaction from making life difficult.)

Similarly, if every time I asked them to do something I got a 'Yes, Dad, no problem, it'd be a pleasure', then I would think I had died and gone to heaven. Can you imagine? Bliss. You really do have to be dogged, determined and most of all believe in yourself, in order to resist the temptation to give in and opt for the easy life.

A few years ago now, Melanie and I took Jack and Sam to Holland for a long weekend to visit some friends. It was an exciting trip, since it was our first time abroad with the children and the first time with them on an aeroplane, too. Our friends were living in a fantastic traditional Dutch town house near Amsterdam, right beside a large canal with big old barges sailing past the front door. Everybody cycled around the narrow cobbled streets on big heavy bikes and you could buy local cheese from the shop round the corner.

The only problem with all this excitement came when bedtime arrived on the first night. Getting young kids to bed in a strange place can be difficult at the best of times, but Jack was going through a particularly challenging phase. Generally, our kids have been excellent sleepers, but it was clear from the start that getting him off to sleep this time was not going to be simple. It wasn't helped by the fact he had only recently moved out of a cot to a bed and was rather enjoying the newfound ability to get out of bed and pootle off to wherever he liked. Also, Sam and Jack were sharing a room for the first time.

However, we carried out our usual routine of bathing them and putting them to bed at 7 pm. Sam went off like a light, but his elder brother decided that he was having none of it and was up like a shot. When Jack was little, for some strange reason, he would only settle with me, so I was left with the task of trying to get him off to sleep while Melanie sat downstairs with our friends drinking wine as dinner was being prepared. Oh, great!

By eight o'clock, Jack and I had gone through the following routine about 10 times.

- Daddy talks to Jack nicely and tells him it's time for bed.
- Daddy gets Jack in bed, all snugly, and leaves the room, closing door behind him.
- Daddy stands halfway down stairs listening to check Jack has gone to sleep.
- Daddy hears various rustling and bumping noises.
- Daddy goes back into bedroom.

- Daddy finds Jack on other side of bedroom poking his brother.

Now, by this time, dinner was ready and being kept warm in the oven, my wife was making pretty large inroads into my share of the wine and I was getting just a tad annoyed. Our friends said I should just give up and Jack could sit with us while we all had dinner, which was incredibly tempting.

However, in the back of my mind was a similar situation about a year earlier, back at home, when Jack had woken in the middle of the night and refused to go back to sleep. Being the world's worst person when woken up in the middle of the night, I took the easy option and brought him into bed with us. After that it took about a fortnight to get him back to his normal habit of sleeping through the night. I wasn't going to go through that again.

So I kept going, and after another 20 minutes or so the little darling finally nodded off and we got to have a proper, grown-up meal all by ourselves.

There could well have been quicker ways to get the same result, but in the end it worked. And it was in the end. I can vividly remember shutting the bedroom door for the umpteenth time wondering just how long this was going to on for, but being determined that I was not going to be the one to give in. And I guess that's the key point. From an incredibly early age children learn to push you all the time in order to see where the boundaries are and to see what's set in stone and what's negotiable: how many stories can I get before I have to go to bed; how loud can I shout before I'm told to be quiet; how hard can I hit my brother before I'm told off; did Dad really mean it when he said next time I pull the dog's tail I go straight to bed; what happens if I only pull Rover's tail a little bit this time?

And it's a characteristic that stays with us all. Everybody knew at school who were the teachers for whom you had to get your homework done and who were the ones who would let you get away with it. I had a teacher who had a little toy koala bear that he clipped to the side of his blackboard. If you went into the classroom at the start of the lesson and the bear was at the top of the board you knew he was in a good mood, and the lesson would be quite a laugh. If the bear was at the bottom of the board you knew he wasn't, and it wouldn't be. We were terrified of him, though he never had to raise his voice. There were other teachers, though, who could shout and rant all they wanted, but nobody was that bothered.

And this ability shows up in our work lives, too. How many times have you heard, or been involved in, a conversation like the following?

'So what's Manager X like to work for?'

'Oh, he's fine – doesn't get in the way much, lets you do your own thing, doesn't know what I'm up to half the time.'

'Not like your old Manager Y, then?'

'Oh, no – she was always keeping tabs on us, couldn't get a thing passed her, always seemed to ask the pertinent question. Got things done, mind.'

As a manager, therefore, you will constantly be tested by people to see where your boundaries lie and whether or not you stand by what you say. So that strategy you set, be it for a small day-to-day task or a long-term corporate programme, will be challenged and tested, even if you don't realise it. If you're not prepared to stick to it and defend it against such tests, your credibility as a leader will quickly disappear.

The interesting thing with children, according to the experts, is that they actually need to know where the boundaries lie. Ironically, if, when the parent is tested in the sorts of ways I described above, they don't respond in a consistent way and make it clear to the child how far they can go, then the child gets confused and in the long run their behaviour deteriorates. According to Professor Robert Winston, a leading fertility expert and presenter of the BBC's *Child of Our Time*, one of the causes of unruly behaviour in older children is a lack of discipline in their earlier years. I'm not saying that if you don't stick to your strategy people are going to start firing pea shooters at you and putting whoopee cushions on your executive chair, but getting things done will get harder and harder.

> AS A MANAGER, YOU WILL CONSTANTLY BE TESTED BY PEOPLE TO SEE WHERE YOUR BOUNDARIES LIE.

One of the things I've found when bringing up three boys, though, is that, while discipline is very important, if you picked up on absolutely everything that went on you would spend the whole time saying, 'Don't do this, don't do that, no, no, get down, be quiet, don't be rude' and so forth. Life would become one long episode of repeated negativity. Sometimes it is actually better to concede some ground rather than put up a fight every time a challenge is made.

You need to be pragmatic and choose your battles, not least because so much negativity becomes tiresome for everybody. Also, it means that when you do decide it's time for a battle, the point is made much more effectively than if it's lost in an ongoing moan. I've found that it's also not necessarily a case of picking up on the worst offence, more a case of realising when there's a specific point of principle at stake, or showing that a boundary has been reached, or crossed.

As a manager you need to decide when challenges to your strategy do occur, whether they are serious enough to dig your heels in over, or whether there are mitigating circumstances that mean it might be better to let it go in this instance. Sometimes there are perfectly good business reasons why it's better for you to back off. Or it can be a case of ongoing 'bargaining': 'OK, I'll let them have their way on this one, but I'll make sure they do what I want next week when I know there's something more important coming up.'

As I said, it's down to judgement, and only you can make that decision. While there aren't any magic answers, what I do find helpful is putting myself in the shoes of the person who is challenging me. If I let this one go, are they going to respect me for making a pragmatic call, or are they going to go, 'Phew – got away with that one'? If you can get the answer right you've got it sussed.

At the end of the day your strategy stays the same – you're just steering a pragmatic course in the short term to make sure you defend it the best you can in the long term.

... Unless You Need to Change It

'A fanatic is one who can't change his mind and won't change the subject.'

Winston Churchill

IT is important, though, to be able to recognise when a strategy isn't working. For some people, this can be just as hard as it is for others to stick to a strategy. And, the higher the level the strategy is at, the harder it is to swallow pride and admit it isn't working. We've all heard about big projects that carried on and on, costing more and more, because they were always 'nearly there', but never actually were, and no one had the guts to say enough was enough and pull the plug. If you find yourself in this situation, it may be best to change the strategy after all.

Be careful, though. What I'm *not* talking about is giving in when the first challenge is made and somebody disagrees with what you are doing or refuses to follow your direction. What I *am* talking about is when you've been trying your approach for some time and there is objective evidence to show that it isn't working and that the results you are aiming for just aren't coming. It's clearly a matter of judgement, but it is crucial that you should be able to make that judgement and understand when it is the right time to try something different.

Children are experts at this. Our children like sweets – surprise, surprise! Fortunately they are still at an age when the concepts of money and sweetshops are beyond them, so supply is still within our control, aided by a high shelf in our kitchen. Demand, on the other hand, is out of control. The children will periodically (every five minutes on a good day) ask me if they can have something from the sweetie jar. Now, if I say no, which I'm inclined to do, do they say, 'OK, then, Dad, I accept your decision, they're not good for me anyway and will only mean I will suffer at the hands of the dentist in future years'? Oh, no. They go and find their mum and ask again. If they can work it, they will try to make sure she didn't hear the original request, because this has more chance of leading to a positive result.

And, if Nanna is staying for the weekend, they don't bother to come to me or Melanie at all. My mother couldn't say no to her three perfectly formed grandchildren if they asked her to drive the getaway car while they robbed the local bank. They all worked out at a pretty early age (two) that, if they ask Nanna for something, the success rate is somewhere in the region of 100 per cent – a bit higher if they do something cute a few minutes beforehand. Kids are experts at devising strategies and using them until they stop working, at which point they try something else.

Unfortunately, this skill doesn't necessarily stay with us as we grow older. A highly paid trainer on a development course I once attended described the inability to change a strategy as 'fly syndrome'. Flies don't like being indoors and on finding themselves in such a predicament do their best to get back outdoors. Flies know that outdoors is all bright and sunny with blue sky (occasionally) and indoors isn't, so they head for the bright, sunny bit. Unfortunately, nobody has explained the concept of glass windows to the fly community. Invariably the fly will encounter a pane of the stuff while heading for the bright, sunny bit and get confused. 'The bright, sunny bit is right there, but I can't seem to get to it,' says the fly. 'I'll give it another shot.' And so on and so on and so on, until someone comes along and

> **UNDERSTAND WHEN IT IS THE RIGHT TIME TO TRY SOMETHING DIFFERENT.**

kills it with a rolled-up copy of the *Daily Mail* because they've got fed up with the thing buzzing about and banging its head against the window for the past 45 minutes. The point? Don't be a fly.

Take Your Team with You

'I always knew you had personality. The doctor said it was hyperactivity, but I knew better.'

Homer Simpson (to Bart), *The Simpsons*

KNOWING where you want to take your team is only half the story, though. There's also a journey to go on and people, having decided that they will go on it with you, must be prepared to stay with you. After all, people don't have to cooperate. Just like the child who decides to run away from home when things aren't working out, employees can easily decide you're not the manager they want to work for and either leave of their own accord, or, often worse, stay and make life difficult for you.

Getting people to want to work for you puts you in a much better position than if you need to *force* people to work for you. In *Raising Happy Children*, Jan Parker and Jan Stimpson talk about the fact that, if you can get parenting right, your children, rather than fearing punishment like prisoners obeying their guards, will instead develop an attachment and regard for you that means they will want to please you. If you can get management right, the same can be said of your team.

But what makes people decide you are the manager they want to work for, that they are going to become 'attached' to you, and that they're going to go on that journey with you?

Integrity

'The superior man understands what is right; the inferior man understands what will sell.'

Confucius, Chinese thinker and social philosopher

THE crucial word for me when you talk about leaders and leadership is *integrity*. Integrity is an easy word to say, but a harder one to define, and even harder to learn, maybe even impossible. But we all know it when we see it.

Looking up the word *integrity* on the thesaurus Mr Gates has kindly supplied on my PC produces the following results:

    honesty
    virtue
    honour
    morality
    principle
    uprightness
    righteousness
    goodness

As I say, a difficult set of things to learn – a pretty impressive list of words by anybody's standards. There can't be many people who get an A grade in each one of *that* lot.

What are important, though, are your values and ethics. These can be derived from all sorts of sources and can cover all sorts of subjects at all sorts of levels. What is your attitude to the environment? Do you tolerate inaccurate work? How do you treat employees from other races? Do you always put yourself first? Do you contribute generously to leaving presents? Would you turn a blind eye to an exaggerated expense claim? Do you favour people who went to your university? And so on. They can range from the minor to the fundamental. Your team, though, will pick up on where you stand and decide (a) whether or not they like and respect your stance and (b) what your stance means in terms of how they are going to have to operate on a daily basis. Knowing what your 'immovables' are will mean they will know what you expect of them.

In their book *Leadership and the Quest for Integrity*, Joseph L. Badaracco Jr and Richard R. Ellsworth (they're from Harvard Business School so they must be clever) interviewed a number of CEOs of a variety of leading US companies about leadership. When they asked them the question, 'What personal values are more likely to lead to outstanding managerial performance?' one of the top responses was 'a strong set of personal ethical standards' – principally, honesty and fairness:

> *Again and again, executives told us that these characteristics are the fundamental source of trust and loyalty in an organization. They believed that the widely accepted conflict between high ethical values and economical performance was, in the long-term, a false dichotomy. Such ethical values lie at the heart of the organizations these leaders had spent much of their careers trying to create.*

The interesting thing about values is that not only are they a key part of gaining the respect and support of the people you are managing, but, if they are clear enough and strong enough and your team members agree with them, they become a management system in themselves. A shared set of values is far stronger and more powerful than a set of systems or structures aimed at motivating people to work in the way that you want them to. You can write procedural documents until you're blue in the face (and I have) in order to try to get people to follow common processes and methods, but, at the end of the day, they are never completely watertight and there's always somebody who hasn't read the procedure and does the 'wrong' thing. Somebody once told me that the only reasons for writing procedures were that you either don't trust people or you think they're incompetent.

For parents, values are also important. We spend the first few years of our children's lives almost literally watching over everything they do and every step they make. However, at some point you have to start to let go. When Jack started school, it was very strange to think that he was running around in the playground each day, making friends, losing friends, playing games and so on, all pretty much by himself, when only four years earlier I was having to pop my head round the nursery door before I went to bed just to check that the newly arrived bundle of joy was still breathing!

> IF YOUR VALUES ARE CLEAR ENOUGH AND STRONG ENOUGH, THEY BECOME A MANAGEMENT SYSTEM IN THEMSELVES.

It's amazing how they go from total dependence on you to making their first steps in the world on their own. And as they get older, bit by bit, you have to let go more and more and leave them to it. By the time they're teenagers you're lucky to get a look in, other than the odd request for a tenner and a lift to the pub.

As this process develops, the opportunities for you to impart direct discipline, knowledge and wisdom diminish more and more. You can't be there the whole time saying, 'Johnny, no, don't pick your nose, don't hit Freddy, don't leave your room in a mess, don't mix your drinks, don't do drugs, don't mug that old lady.' More and more, it's up to them to decide themselves what's right and wrong, what's good for them and what's bad for them, what's acceptable and what's unacceptable. The reference point they use when doing this is the values that have been in place while you have been in a position to exert direct influence over them. They may choose to ignore those values – there are plenty of people around who have rebelled against their parents, if only for the sake of it – but those values will be the reference point. For example, if you've always insisted that hygiene is important, this will be a factor in the development, or otherwise, of the nose-picking habit.

Similarly, in the workplace, it is your values that will guide your team as they go about their daily tasks. You can't be directly managing your team the whole time and constantly influencing them to do their work in exactly the way you would like. If this were the case, there would be no point in your having a team at all and you might as well do all their work yourself. If they share in your values, however, they will be working almost as if they were you (now there's a scary thought!).

Shared values can also be a powerful motivator, more so than money. One of the things that have always grated on me hugely is when I've attended training courses on corporate finance and some smug tutor in a smart suit stands up and kicks off the session with the question, 'What is the purpose of any company?' Delegates always come up with answers along the lines of 'to produce products, to serve customers, to develop new technology, to improve standards of living, to provide good jobs for its employees' and so on. And what does the smug tutor in the suit do? He looks even more smug and says, 'No, it's to make money for its shareholders.' The subsequent debates I've had with some of these guys have lasted for hours. Now I recognise the importance of shareholder returns, but I do not go to work every day thinking I must make money for our shareholders, and I certainly don't go to work every day thinking I must make sure my team understands how important it is that we make money for our shareholders.

If financial performance is the only value that is in place then you're going to lose people's support very quickly. The sorts of values that are important to people are, in fact, linked to many of the answers above. People want to take pride in their work and produce products and services that are outstanding in some way. They want to carry out work that helps them develop their skills and challenges them. People want to work with others they respect and trust and want to be treated fairly and honestly. People want to know their efforts make a difference and that their time on the job has been worthwhile.

Obviously, people recognise that the company must be financially viable and they want to be paid well (I've got a wife and three kids to support, after all!). However, if I had to work in a company, and for a manager, whose values were centred on economic performance, or a company and a manager whose values were centred on producing outstanding products, developing my skills and ensuring my efforts make a difference, then I know which I would plump for. The thing is, of course, if these sorts of values are in place, then the economic performance follows automatically.

Making sure your team understand, and as far as possible share, your values is a central part of being seen as somebody who has high integrity and, as a result, is a strong manager. In a survey of office workers, 85 per cent said that values based on honesty and strong ethics were an important part of management. Only 40 per cent said that these values were in place with their own managers. Make sure you are not in the 60 per cent.

Setting an Example

> 'The example of great and pure individuals is the only thing
> that can lead us to noble thoughts and deeds.'
>
> Albert Einstein

IT'S the classic line from parent to child: 'Do as I say, not as I do.'
Well, forget it. Saying this has no effect whatsoever – with your
kids or with your team. At the end of the day, what you do counts
far more than what you say.

Children learn by watching you. What you do and how you
behave in situations is all absorbed from an incredibly early age,
even when your behaviour is incredibly subtle. Jack demonstrated
this to us perfectly when he was about six months old. By this age
we had managed to get him sleeping through the night fairly
routinely. In fact we were feeling pretty pleased that the various
techniques we had employed over the previous months to get him
sleeping through were paying off. At last we felt we were starting
to emerge from the bewilderment that surrounds the arrival of
your first child. Life was starting to return to some sort of
normality, or at least something that we were gaining some degree
of control over again.

In fact, we were feeling so confident we decided it was time to
venture out of the house again, all on our own, and go for a meal
out. Melanie's parents were staying one weekend, so it seemed the
perfect opportunity for them to start to hone their babysitting
skills and for us to spend a Saturday evening at a decent local
restaurant. The table was booked.

That evening Jack was fed, bathed and put to bed at seven o'clock
on the dot, in exactly the same way as he had been for all of his
short life. We thought we were pretty relaxed about the whole

thing. We were going to be out until 11, and Jack hadn't woken up before then for months and had, anyway, been sleeping through the whole night now for several weeks. Melanie's parents had stayed many times before and were no strangers to watching *Emmerdale* while keeping one ear on the baby monitor for any sounds of disgruntlement. The mobile-phone batteries were charged and we could get back pretty quickly if need be. We were both looking forward to a pleasant few hours back in the real world. Off we went.

The meal was excellent. The starter went down nicely. The main course was turning out to be pretty tasty, too. Halfway through, I remember thinking that we should move the mobile phone from between the condiments, switch it off and put it away. There was no way it was going to be necessary. Jack hadn't been awake at this time since he was about three months old. We should just forget about home life for a while and enjoy being just the two of us again. No sooner had I thought such crazy thoughts than – *beep, beep, beep*. The phone rang (polyphonic ringtones of the theme tune to *The Archers* weren't around in those days).

My salmon and vegetables, kissed with a tangy dill sauce, were rudely interrupted by the news that our son had been wailing for the past half-hour and that nothing Grandma or Granddad had tried to do to settle him down was working. The bill was hurriedly paid, coats were fetched and we were back home within 10 minutes. In another five, Melanie had settled Jack and he was fast asleep back in his cot. I was tempted to suggest we get back in the car and go and find out if the remainder of my salmon was retrievable, or whether it had already found its way to the bin. I decided I was wasting my time.

Now, I'm not naïve enough to say that there wouldn't have been a little bit of apprehension around when Jack was put to bed that night. But we genuinely were pretty relaxed about it. It was the first time he had been left with anybody else, but we were very confident that he would sleep through the whole thing oblivious of anything that was different from every other night. However, what little apprehension there was he obviously picked up on. There can't have been much, but he sensed it, and it obviously unsettled him.

I often wondered afterwards whether this was really the case or just an unfortunate coincidence that Jack happened to pick the night we were out to play up. A few years later, though, I was in no doubt when a very similar thing happened with Will.

As children get older this ability to sense what their parents are feeling and to react accordingly continues to develop. If you take your kids to the swimming pool for the first time and you're apprehensive about water then they will pick up on it and share your nervousness. I've seen it happen. If you are wary about certain people and feel uncomfortable in their company, then your children will too. They are constantly looking to you for the cue as to how to react to different situations, especially new ones. Your signs, however subtle, will strongly influence their response. Even when children are at an age where rebellious streaks start to appear, they still look to their parents for an example of what is acceptable and what isn't.

Sam likes to help out when I'm doing DIY. I'll be there, banging nails into a stud partition wall, and he'll be beside me with his plastic hammer, viciously pummelling a spare piece of wood (or his brother, whichever is closer). I was working on a new bathroom when he had not been long talking. Now, I'm not a prolific swearer, but I do tend to let out the odd 'bugger' when something goes wrong with my pretty amateurish DIY. After a few afternoons of helping me out, we discovered that Sam's new favourite word was, you've guessed it, 'bugger'. There he was, this two-and-a-half-year-old, at his toddler group having trouble getting his teddies to sit up properly and he would let out a loud and crisp 'bugger'. I stopped, and fortunately, after a while so, did he, but it was a bit embarrassing when people asked how his speech was coming along: 'Oh, he's saying five words now: mummy, daddy, cat, dog and bugger.'

So if young children, even six-month-old babies, have an acute ability to observe and react to the example set by their parents, just imagine how important the example you set to your team is as a manager. The trendy management term for this is 'walking the talk' – what you say is also what you do. If one of your values is hard work and you expect your team to buy into this, then don't be surprised if they're reluctant when you spend most of your time drinking coffee and standing around chatting. If you come down hard on them when approving their expenses but they know that you're spending company money on lavish dinners and hotels, then your credibility and integrity are not going to remain intact for long.

Consistency is also key here. If people see you behaving differently – depending on your mood, for example – then again your integrity is going to suffer. If your values and your own associated behaviour are only optional, then nobody is going to respect them or you. When you hear people say, 'You can always depend on Joe Bloggs', you interpret it as a positive statement. However, 'You can rely on Joe Bloggs 80 per cent of the time' doesn't have anything like the same impact.

A manager's life is not a private one. Unfortunately, no matter how much you may not want the attention, your team will always be observing you, how you conduct yourself and how you react to specific situations. All the decisions you make will be assessed by people to determine whether they are the 'correct' ones. All your behaviours will be observed and marked off against a mental checklist to see if you measure up. Your team will know where you have your lunch and what time you arrive for work and leave each day. They will know what car you drive and whether you polish your shoes. In *The Way to Win*, Will Carling talks about the last training session

> AT THE END OF THE DAY, WHAT YOU DO COUNTS FAR MORE THAN WHAT YOU SAY.

before England met Scotland, who had unexpectedly beaten them the year before, in the semifinal of the 1991 Rugby World Cup campaign:

> *Although I focused on the training session itself, my mind kept on drifting to the evening, when I would be speaking at the team meeting. I was desperately trying to find a hook on which to hang my talk, a hook which would trigger the emotion of the squad and create the focused intent that we hadn't achieved eighteen months before.*

> *With the session complete, I wandered off to do the required interviews with the assembled TV crews and waiting media people. As I went back to the changing room, the manager, Geoff Cooke, took me aside and asked, 'How do you feel? Do you think the session went well?' I was overjoyed with the quality of the session, but slightly puzzled by Geoff's question. Why had he asked it?*

> *He explained that my head had been down the whole time. I hadn't made any comment to any of the players during the thirty minutes that we had been running. As a result, the squad had sat in the changing room afterwards trying to work out why I was upset, and what they had done wrong. I had*

underestimated how closely the players observe me and how much they read into my movements and apparent moods during the session. I had provided no encouragement for them.

Spooky as it may feel, it pays to remember that you are being watched by your team, if only subconsciously. It's always a good idea, therefore, to make sure you're walking your own talk.

Trust

DORY: Come on, trust me on this one.
MARLIN: Trust you?
DORY: Yes, trust, it's what friends do.

Finding Nemo (2003)

SMALL children are easy to throw up in the air and catch – and they love it. Well, the three Durston siblings certainly do. I have the bad back to prove it. 'Again, Daddy, again!' they shout as you launch them skywards and catch them on the way back down again. We live in a Victorian house, with high ceilings, so you can get them up really high. They then throw their arms and legs out as if they were flying, their eyes wide with excitement. Their trust is absolute, which is actually quite a nice feeling, but at the same time gives you a huge sense of responsibility.

I hope the boys will always trust me so fully, but I know that, as they get older and their naïvety diminishes, it will need more effort and sound judgement on my part. Trust is such an important part of a parent–child relationship that it's something that you can't afford to lose. Every time you introduce your child to something new, they are basically doing it only because they trust in you and feel safe in the knowledge that they won't get hurt – either physically or emotionally – and that there must be some good reason why you want them to do whatever it is you are introducing them to. For example, teaching a child to swim means they have to trust that, when they're swimming in the big pool without armbands for the first time, you're not going to let them drown if their doggy paddle lets them down.

Trust also provides the background for an open and honest

relationship with your kids. If they think you're going to fly off the handle at bad news, they're hardly going to come and openly discuss their problems with you. They need to know that they are going to be heard and treated fairly and that you will be able to see their side of the issue. Trust between parents and children is essential.

Similarly, in the workplace, trust is essential for strong leadership and is something that every manager should work hard to develop among their team. If people don't trust you or your judgement, they're unlikely to follow your strategic direction and willingly become a loyal team member. A lack of trust can make people suspicious and liable to work against you rather than for you. At the very least, it means that people are

> **THE PROBLEM WITH TRUST FOR ANY NEW MANAGER IS THAT YOU HAVE TO EARN IT.**

not going to be giving you their best. In the way that a lack of parental trust prevents children from sharing bad news, a lack of managerial trust means that you are at risk of being shielded from bad news. And, believe me, it's the bad news you *want* your team to be telling you, otherwise you can't do your job.

The Chinese have a particularly interesting way of testing trust in their business relationships. I was in Beijing a couple of years ago, meeting the management of some Chinese companies that we are interested in working with. I was visiting with some French, German and Spanish colleagues and after a long day of formal meetings we were told by out hosts that it was time for dinner. We were taken to a very posh company dining room and treated to an extraordinary spread of Chinese cooking that puts our local takeaway to shame.

After several minutes of polite Euro–Sino chitchat, the waitress came round and poured everybody a full glass of red wine. Nothing unusual there. The managing director of the company then proceeded to tell us how much importance the Chinese put on trust and how they saw it as a key part of choosing whom they do business with. All very admirable, I thought. He continued to tell us that the traditional Chinese way of understanding how much trust existed between two parties was to drink together. Even better, I thought. The Chinese logic, he said, was that the only time people truly open up and are honest with each other is after a few drinks. If somebody, therefore, is not prepared to drink with you, then they're not to be trusted.

As I pondered this, the MD then picked up his large glass of red wine, exclaimed in perfect English, 'Chin, chin!' and downed it in one! What was worse, as the waitress scurried to his side and refilled his glass, he then looked straight at me. Now, as my wife and friends will testify, while I enjoy the odd tipple, hardened drinking has never been one of my strong points, and the arrival of three children has not exactly increased my tolerance levels. The headline in the next edition of the company magazine flashed before me: AIRBUS FAILS IN CHINA AS DURSTON PROVES HE'S A LIGHTWEIGHT. I picked up my glass and thought of England. We visited four different companies during the seven days we were in China. By the end of the week, I was begging to come home! Fortunately, though, the trip was a success.

As the Chinese obviously understand, the problem with trust for any new manager is that you have to earn it. It's people's natural reaction to mistrust anything or anybody new, so you're starting with zero credit in the bank. In order to develop some trust, the first thing you need to do is get a few things right. Easier said than done, I know, but if people see that your judgement is sound and you're not leading them on a wild-goose chase, their trust in you will start to grow. And, even if you get some things wrong, if you handle the situation appropriately – for example, by admitting to mistakes rather than trying to blame somebody else – people will respect you for it. This bond of trust will grow stronger if you behave with consistency, keep your promises and treat your team with fairness and respect.

All of this will take time. Good management, like good parenting, is a long-term commitment.

Courage

'It is awfully hard to be b-b-brave, when you are only a Very Small Animal.'

Piglet, *Winnie-the-Pooh*

BEFORE I became a father, I never thought that courage would be one of the things that would be high on the list of required attributes. An ability to cope with gratuitous amounts of excrement or the need for an endless supply of cash, maybe, but not courage. It didn't take long to realise that it was something that would need to be mustered much more frequently than I had previously thought. Maybe not courage in the Sir Edmund Hilary or Neil Armstrong sense of the word, but in more of an emotional, sensitive kind of way (I'm such a man of the nineties).

Now getting babies to sleep through the night is high on the list of any new parent's priorities. I am terrible at coping with sleep deprivation, so it was definitely at the top of my list from Day One. In the world of parenting in the twenty-first century, the whole subject is actually surprisingly quite contentious. To simplify the matter hugely, there are two schools of thought. One is based on 'demand-feeding' babies. In other words, whenever they cry for milk you give them some, or if they cry for attention you give them some. The philosophy is that the baby knows what it wants and needs and you should meet its demands when they're made, without any hesitation, no matter what the time of day – or night. The second school of thought is that babies need a routine and, by following a strict timetable of feeding and sleeping, the baby will benefit from the predictability and security of doing the same thing at the same time each day. There are books written on the different approaches by rival authors who are pitched against each other in the 'parenting media' in an almost Wenger-versus-Ferguson type of rivalry. It's all very exciting.

Now I'm not going to advise you on which approach is better. There are certainly varying degrees between these two extremes, and probably other completely different methods too. I'm afraid I'm going to be very liberal and say it's up to parents to decide what is most suited to them. We did that, and decided on an approach based on

> # DIFFICULT AND UNPOPULAR DECISIONS NEED TO BE MADE.

some degree of routine. With a background in project management, it was hard to resist! We haven't been anything like as strict about it as the books suggest, but we have definitely found that a routine has worked well with all three boys.

The problem with the method, though, comes when the little blighters don't do as they're supposed to. Especially at night. It's all very well saying that they need to stick to a routine, but, unfortunately, they do have minds of their own – rather cunning ones at that. If they are supposed to be sleeping and they wake up, then the advice is to employ the technique of 'controlled crying'. Basically, rather than rush straight to them to pamper and cuddle them, you ignore their crying. If they are ill you do relax the rule and if they are crying for extended periods you go in to them every 10 minutes, for a couple of minutes, to reassure them and then leave them to it again until they settle. This sounds very harsh. And it is.

It does work, though. With Jack we had to do very little of this, since he was a good sleeper right from the start, and when we did need to 'do' controlled crying we were pretty rigorous about it. With Sam, however, we were far less so. With two children around, you don't have the luxury of being able to focus on one of them and their routine in the same way as with the firstborn. More importantly, though, whenever Sam cried we were really worried that he would wake up Jack, leaving us with two wailing children on our hands. We were therefore far more inclined to go straight in to him and settle him back to sleep than we ever were with Jack. The problem with this was that, after nine months, Sam was still waking up frequently in the night, whereas Jack at the same age had been sleeping through the night from seven till seven – no problems. We were knackered.

We spoke to our health visitor, who told us that basically Sam was wrapping us around his little finger and that we needed to do some proper controlled crying and run the risk that Jack might be disturbed. We did. Jack didn't stir once. After a week and a half of Sam's wailing every night, sometimes for up to a couple of hours (we were going in to him briefly every 10 minutes, I hasten to add), he finally slept through the whole night for the first time without stirring. And he has done so ever since.

It all sounds very easy now as I write it down. A week and half isn't very long, and, compared with the previous nine months of being woken every night, it wasn't. But leaving Sam to cry like that definitely took some courage. It's a very unnatural thing to leave what on the surface is a very vulnerable bundle of helplessness to scream his head off continuously. Melanie and I would be there, two o'clock in the morning, sitting up in bed, waiting, agonisingly, for the digital clock on the clock/radio to reach the next 10-minute mark so that one of us could go in to Sam and feel a bit more like a proper parent for a couple of brief moments. It was excruciating. In the end, it definitely turned out to be the right thing to do, but at the time it didn't feel that way and we had no idea how long it was going to go on for.

But being a parent so often means that you have to have the courage to do what you believe to be right when not knowing for certain if it is. Deciding whether your children should be given the MMR vaccine, for example; letting your children go to parties when you know there will be plenty of drink and drugs available; or continuing to send them to school when you know they're being bullied – all of these take huge amounts of courage.

In the workplace, the need for courage might not be so personal, but it is very much part of leading and taking decisions that affect your team and the direction you're all going in. Going along with the status quo and taking the easy path is not what leadership is all about. Difficult and unpopular decisions need to be made.

In *Leadership and the Quest for Integrity*, Joseph L. Badaracco Jr and Richard R. Ellsworth write,

> *Yet leadership remains uncommon. Why? Very often the main problem is simply a lack of courage. Not the valor of grand heroic acts, but determination and honesty practiced daily in the small situations and familiar dilemmas of managerial life; the courage to do and say what one believes to be right, rather than what is convenient, familiar or popular; the courage to act on one's vision for his or her organization.*

Leaders who stand out above the rest are the ones who have made truly courageous decisions when they can't possibly be guaranteed of a positive outcome – Winston Churchill on the D-Day landings, John F. Kennedy during the Cuban missile crisis. Courage in management is courage of a lesser degree than this, but it is an integral part of leadership as a manager nonetheless.

Taking decisions that maintain the status quo and just keep things ticking along is easy. Taking ones that change things and have a direct impact on people are not so straightforward. You may have heard of the A380, a pioneering aeroplane we've been building at

Airbus, with which I have been lucky enough to be involved. Everything about it is impressive: it's nearly the length of a football pitch, it weighs well over 500 tonnes, it is as tall as a 12-storey building, it can seat over 800 people on two decks and yet is still the quietest and most fuel-efficient aircraft of its type to date. But it's not just in engineering terms that it is so awe-inspiring: the financial figures are mind-boggling too. At a few hundred million dollars each, they're not cheap to buy. The development programme has cost billions of dollars, and, as you may have also heard, has not all been plain sailing. Now tell me that the person who decided to give the go-ahead to the A380 programme wasn't a courageous person and that they won't be getting a better night's sleep after the programme has paid for itself.

This may be at the extreme end of management decisions, but there are plenty of decisions at a lower level that still require guts:

- Do I select company A to do the work or company B?
- Do I need to make redundancies to keep the business viable?
- Do I offer the inexperienced graduate the job?
- Do I implement a new IT system or make do with the old one?

Unfortunately, there are often no right or wrong answers to such questions, but you can guarantee that, to get anywhere close to the right one, you're going to have to make brave decisions. Do your homework, and be bold.

Humour

'A sense of humour is part of the art of leadership, of getting along with people, of getting things done.'

Dwight D. Eisenhower, 34th President of the USA

I always thought a 'good sense of humour' (or GSOH if you're such a dedicated employee that you have to read the lonely-hearts ads), was a managerial trait that was a bit of a nice-to-have – something that you sometimes see in managers but is there as a bit of a coincidence or accident. That was until I read an article in the *Harvard Business Review*. The gist was that a sense of humour is actually a major characteristic of a good manager. What's more, a 'scientific' experiment was carried out to prove it. The heads of various companies were given an interview – just a general interview on themselves, their work, their company and so forth. During the interview, somebody marked down every time they made a 'joke' – not a 'why did the chicken cross the road?' type of joke, but some sort of off-the-cuff quip or one-liner that added no factual information to the conversation and whose only purpose was to make the interviewer laugh. A whole bunch of these interviews were carried out and a graph of 'number of jokes' versus 'financial strength of company' was plotted. And – lo and behold! – there was a correlation! The heads of the more successful companies made more jokes than the heads of the less successful ones, almost, it seemed, without fail.

After I read the article, I started to look around at managers I worked with and was actually quite surprised at just how often they did use humour. In fact 'witty banter', of varying degrees of quality, was, it turned out, almost a constant part of my working day.

I think there are a few reasons for this. First, making working life fun is a big motivator. We'll look at this in more detail later. Second, humour can be used incredibly effectively to diffuse difficult situations. This was demonstrated in a meeting I attended that was really getting very fraught and emotions were starting to run quite high. A particularly vociferous Frenchman was getting rather angry in a way that only a Frenchman knows how. I was certainly not at all envious of the English manager who was chairing the meeting and was trying to keep things moving forward in a constructive and positive way. I don't remember the detail of what was said, but, during an especially aggressive torrent of expletives by said Frenchman, the chairman stepped in with a witty one-liner that was rather amusing: something along the lines of suggesting that the meeting should have been held at Waterloo! Instantly, the atmosphere changed as everybody, including, to his credit, the Frenchman, had a good laugh. The issue was sorted out and the meeting moved on amicably.

Humour is an important part of reaching and being 'accepted' by other people. If you make people laugh, they see you as human and one of them – on the same wavelength. If you're a bit dull and bland, you're more likely to be considered an outsider – somebody who's not completely human, no matter how technically brilliant you might be.

The danger here, though, is that humour can't really be learned and is an incredibly subtle ability with all sorts of boundaries, cultural nuances and social considerations that have to be respected and observed. You can't just turn up at a meeting having read a Bernard Manning joke book the night before and expect to have people eating out of your hand. Ricky Gervais, as David Brent in the British sitcom *The Office*, provides the perfect example of how a manager who thinks he's funny, but isn't, is actually far worse than a manager with no sense of humour at all.

What it does mean, though, is that you shouldn't be afraid of 'having a laugh' as a manager. Obviously, you need to be a good judge of what is acceptable and what isn't, but at the same time you don't have to be, indeed *shouldn't* be, a bore who never utters anything other than financial figures or items on action lists. If we never cracked jokes with our kids or

> YOU SHOULDN'T
> BE AFRAID OF
> 'HAVING A LAUGH'
> AS A MANAGER.

had a laugh with them, we know intuitively that we'd soon lose their interest, and getting them to do any of the more serious stuff would be hard work. There aren't many kids in the school playground who say, 'My dad's the best because he gets me to do times tables the whole time.' There are probably a few more, though, who say, 'My dad's the best because he's really funny and makes me laugh.'

Assertive or Aggressive?

MOTHER: Darling, I employed the last nanny because I thought she would be strict with the children. She seemed so cross and angry.

FATHER: Darling, don't confuse efficiency with a liver complaint.

Mr and Mrs Banks, *Mary Poppins* (1964)

THE problem with children is that they have minds of their own. As you may have realised by now, I spent the first couple of years of my children's lives nurturing them in any way possible in order to maximise the amount of shut-eye I was able to snatch, but once they reached the age of two the focus changed in a marked way. The obsession with sleep (or lack of it) turned to an obsession with behaviour.

This stage is not called the 'terrible twos' for nothing. What is remarkable is the speed of the transformation. Almost overnight, your chubby little bundle of innocence, naïvety and loveliness that trots about the house with cute little steps, gurgling 'Mama' and 'Dada', turns into chubby bundle from hell. I don't think anything can properly prepare a parent for the first tantrum. Usually it happens in the most inconvenient of places – the supermarket, a wedding, Grandma's living room – all strategically chosen to inflict maximum embarrassment. The waterworks are turned on, the shouting begins, the feet are stomped, the screaming from deep within is turned up to full volume and the blood vessels in the face are strained to bursting point. Welcome to the next 14 years of being a parent.

Fortunately, toddler tantrums don't last for ever. It just feels like it at the time. However, challenging behaviour, of varying degrees, does. It is something that becomes part of everyday life.

I'm sure there are some little angels out there who do exactly as they're told all of the time. Unfortunately, with three boys, this has never been a feature in our household. Every day, as a parent you are tested. This behaviour, and how to react to it, is something every parent needs to deal with. They can do so in various ways:

Some parents deal with it aggressively. Lots of shouting, intimidation, anger and sometimes smacking. Surprisingly, some children actually do respond to this approach, seeing the attention as a sign of their parents' love. Certainly, from a discipline point of view, it can be effective, though the obedience that results is one that is based on fear, not respect, and the child can end up being frightened and intimidated or rebellious and defiant – or a mixture of the two.

Aggression tends to breed aggression. When disciplining Jack soon after it first became necessary to do so, I remember crouching down to look him sternly in the eye and shouting at him about something particularly unpleasant he had done. It turned out to be a complete waste of time. All he did was shout back at me. I soon realised that shouting was going to get me nowhere.

At the other end of the scale, some parents remain passive towards the bad behaviour. The child is basically given a free rein to do what they like and 'express' themselves rather than be tied down and inhibited by rules, regulations and discipline. As a result the parents can often feel, and be, walked over while the children run amok doing whatever they like. This approach, more often than not, is not a conscious decision but a result of timidity or shyness on the part of the parents, who do not have the confidence to exert their will on their children. And the children don't respond well to it themselves.

In between being aggressive and being passive is being assertive. I'm sure it will be of no surprise that it is this approach that is commonly agreed to be the most appropriate when dealing with errant children. In his book *The Secret of Happy Children*, Steve Biddulph says,

> *Assertive parents are clear, firm, determined and, on the inside, confident and relaxed. Their children learn that what Mum or Dad says goes but, at the same time, that they will not be treated with put-downs or humiliation.*

Being an assertive parent means letting the child know that, once they've crossed a boundary, their behaviour is unacceptable and there are certain rules that you and society expect them to live within. It's not about shouting or intimidation, but about using a firm voice and firm body language. It's about letting them know when you mean business and that you won't be moved on certain issues. Sometimes there is no debate (believe me, entering into a debate with a six-year-old can be incredibly dangerous – I've tried it, and lost). It's about communicating a message in clear and unambiguous terms, making sure they understand it, and being persistent in making sure that they comply, be it a case of their tidying up their toys, saying sorry when they've hit their brother or turning off the TV and going to bed.

Once the child gets the message that you're not going to give up then they (usually) concede and comply. If they spot a chink in your armour then they (always) take advantage of it. When used in the framework of a loving and caring environment where good behaviour is recognised and praised, being assertive with your children when their behaviour isn't so good can be incredibly effective. It just takes a bit of self-control and determination.

For a manger, assertiveness is just as important and can also be incredibly effective – not in terms of dealing with bad behaviour, but in terms of managing people who don't always want to do what you want them to do. It's not quite the same as, 'Ah, but Dad, I don't want to go to bed yet', but sometimes it's not all that far off.

The problem at work, though, is that people often confuse being assertive with being aggressive. Everybody is able to recognise passive managers and it is generally accepted that this is a weak approach to management. If people are allowed just to get on with things with no intervention or direction from their manager, then either there is no need for a manager or the manager is taken advantage of and things spiral out of control and end up in a mess. 'Strong' management is therefore often thought to be the opposite – thumping the desk, shouting at people, threatening, bullying, and so forth.

In a factory I once worked at, the managing director of the plant used to get the supervisor of each production line to stand by the end of his line of machines each morning with his staff alongside him. The MD was a big bloke and would tour the factory, stopping off at each supervisor and his collection of workers to review the previous day's output. If there had been any problems or production shortfalls, the offending supervisor would be reprimanded in front of all his staff. Not an understanding, let's-work-it-out-and-resolve-the-problem type of reprimand, but a loud, in-your-face, temper-losing, humiliating type of telling-off. To say that the entire workforce were scared of the guy would be an understatement. It was a classic case of ruling by fear.

As with parenting, this is not necessarily a completely ineffective way of managing people, in that it can get short-term results. However, in the long term, it doesn't get the best out of people and it certainly won't mean that you have the best people working for you – anyone with half an ounce of self-respect is soon going to leave. Also, any problems are going to be hidden well away, and employees soon become resentful. Aggressive managers, like tinpot dictators, are often the most insecure and paranoid because they know that nobody likes them and that they are probably being plotted against. As Tony Blair once said to Michael Howard in Prime Minister's Questions, 'Being nasty is not the same as being effective.'

Being assertive as a manager, therefore, is about being clear about what you want people to do, and communicating this to them in unambiguous terms. It's about listening to people but not getting dragged into a long debate about the whys and wherefores of an issue. As with a parent, it's not about shouting or intimidation, but about using a firm voice and firm body language. It's about being resolute on issues and your ideas, and not being easily made to change your mind or water down your approach in order to try to keep everybody happy.

> AT WORK, PEOPLE OFTEN CONFUSE BEING ASSERTIVE WITH BEING AGGRESSIVE.

Probably most importantly, it's about not being afraid of conflict, but seeing conflict as a perfectly acceptable process to go through to get to the right answer rather than something negative that has to be avoided.

All of this is very easy to say, but for a lot of people much harder actually to carry out, especially if they are afraid of conflict. I come from a family background where conflict was avoided at all cost. In my family you just don't do conflict. Melanie's family, however, are more used to it, which made the top table on our wedding day an interesting place to be! This has meant, though, that I have had to work quite hard at my own assertiveness – I have certainly never been in danger of banging the table too much.

But what I eventually learned was that everybody has a right to their own opinion. This may sound a bit obvious, right on and politically correct, but it is actually a really powerful concept for anybody who is not comfortable with conflict. Once you have understood that you have this right, it makes standing up for your case a lot easier, rather than backing down at the first sign of any resistance. It may mean there are situations where you have to agree to disagree, but it does mean that when conflict arises you have as much right as the other person not to give in and to be the one who comes out on top. As a result, assertiveness becomes easy.

Passion

'We are the music makers, and we are the dreamers of dreams.'

Willy Wonka, *Willy Wonka and the Chocolate Factory* (1971)

IN the way that passion for your kids and family means that you are prepared to do whatever it takes to protect and nurture them, passion for your career enables you to achieve things that at first glance would appear unachievable. A passion for what you do leads to great things; turning up for work each day because it pays the mortgage leads to mediocrity, at best.

True leaders display real passion. They don't need to pretend that what they do is important. What they do is part of them. Apparently, Guy Wenger, brother of the Arsenal football manager Arsène, said his brother was 'only ever going to be involved in football'. The entrepreneur and businessman, Virgin's Richard Branson, was running businesses before most of us had stopped wearing short trousers. These people don't go to work: they are their work.

> **TRUE LEADERS DON'T NEED TO PRETEND THAT WHAT THEY DO IS IMPORTANT.**

A short story:
Three men are working in a quarry. The first is asked, 'What do you do?' 'I hit rocks with a hammer,' he replies. The second is asked the same question. 'I'm making blocks of stone for builders,' he answers. Finally, the third man is asked what he does. 'I am building a cathedral,' he says.

If you're hitting rocks, then maybe it's time to look for something different. If you're building a cathedral, then great.

MOTIVATION

'Motivation is everything. You can do the work of two people, but you can't be two people. Instead, you have to inspire the next guy down the line and get him to inspire his people.'

Lee Iacocca, American industrialist

IF leadership is all about setting a strategy and having the personality traits to take people with you, motivation is what you need to do to make sure that people *want* to be with you. It also ensures that they then stay with you and achieve more while doing it.

There are plenty of managers who believe that motivation is a subject that belongs on some HR course and it is certainly not something that they need to take seriously or be involved with themselves. 'Surely,' they say, 'if people are given a good day's pay, they are obliged to give the company a good day's work.' And to a certain extent they are right. But unfortunately life isn't as simple as that. There are plenty of employees who do perform a fair day's work for a fair day's pay. However, there are also those who don't. No matter which group somebody fits into, though, how much you are able to 'get out of them' will depend on how well you are able to motivate them.

And salary is only the beginning. Every amateur psychologist will know about Maslow's 'hierarchy of needs', which says that every human has varying levels of needs that they require to be fulfilled, and that they cannot move on to the next level till the previous one is in place. After basic physical needs such as food, shelter and clothing, we move on to deeper levels of needs, each becoming more 'emotional' than the previous – safety, love, self-esteem and so on – until finally we reach 'self-actualisation', where we have realised our full potential as a human being and have reached 'self-fulfilment'.

MOTIVATION

In relation to work, this means that our salary, like the food and shelter, is actually only a minimum requirement for people to carry out a 'fair day's work'. On top of this are a whole bunch of other factors to do with social interaction, status, recognition and achievement that are also important. It is these additional items that need to be addressed by motivation.

First, a little story. In his book *The Secret of Happy Children*, Steve Biddulph explains why love is important for children:

> *In 1945, the Second World War ended and Europe lay in ruins. Among the many human problems to be tackled was that of caring for the thousands of orphans whose parents had either been killed or permanently separated from them by the war.*
>
> *The Swiss, who had managed to stay out of the war itself, sent their health workers out to begin tackling some of these problems; one man, a doctor, was given the job of researching how to best care for the orphan babies.*
>
> *He travelled about Europe and visited many kinds of orphan-care situations, to see what was the most successful type of care. He saw many extremes. In some places, American field hospitals had been set up and the babies were snug in stainless steel cots, in hygienic wards, getting their four-hourly feeds of special milk formula from crisply uniformed nurses.*
>
> *At the other end of the scale, in remote mountain villages, a truck had simply pulled up, the driver had asked, 'Can you look after these babies?' and left half a dozen crying infants in the care of the villagers. Here, surrounded by kids, dogs, goats, in the arms of the village women, the babies took their chances on goat's milk and the communal stew pot.*

The Swiss doctor had a simple way of comparing the different forms of care. No need even to weigh the babies, far less measure coordination or look for smiling and eye contact. In those days of influenza and dysentery, he used the simplest of all statistics – the death rate.

And what he discovered was rather a surprise … as epidemics raged through Europe and many people were dying, the children in the rough villages were thriving better than their scientifically-cared-for counterparts in the hospitals!

The doctor had discovered something that old wives had known for a long time but no one had really listened. He had discovered babies need love to live.

The infants in the field hospital had everything but affection and stimulation. The babies in the villages had more hugs, bounces and things to see than they knew what to do with and, given reasonable basic care, were thriving.

Now this is going to sound cheesy. Really cheesy. But motivation of your team, in a way, is equivalent to the love you give a child. (I did warn you!) You can raise a child with all the right kit – house, clothes, food, toys, expensive education – but without love, as the above passage suggests, the child is not going to thrive. Likewise, you can provide your team with great salaries, company cars, nice offices, good expense accounts, but if they're not motivated you're wasting your time.

I don't know about where you work, but I often hear it said, figuratively, that so-and-so needs a bit of a hug or needs to have an arm put round them when things aren't going well. This chapter is about how to do that, without being dismissed for sexual harassment!

Attention

'Why do you always have to be the center of attention?'

Carter, *Power Rangers Light Speed Rescue* (2000)

THE easiest and least complicated way to motivate somebody is quite simply to pay them some attention. I'm not joking. What you say is not particularly important, nor necessarily is how long you spend saying it, as long as it's something. 'Nice weather' or 'How are you?' will do.

People just love attention. Adults and children. Children love attention so much that they will do anything to get some. In fact, if children are not getting enough attention, they would rather be naughty and get told off than be 'good' and be ignored. Not convinced? In *The Secret of Happy Children*, Steve Biddulph also recounts an experiment carried out by child psychologists that helps explain the phenomenon. In the experiment, rats were placed in a special cage, with food, drink and a little lever. The rats ate the food, drank the water and eventually, out of curiosity, pressed the lever. The lever opened a little window in the cage that revealed a film being shown on the wall outside (not sure what films rats like, but obviously in the rat world going to the flicks is seen as a bit of a treat). After a short while the window would close and the rat would have to press the lever again to see some more of the film. During the experiment, it transpired that the rats were very willing to work hard at continually pressing the lever in order to keep the film in view, the conclusion being that intelligent creatures, such as rats and children, like to have something interesting to do.

The experiment didn't stop there, though. Next, the researchers put the same rats into a different cage, with food and drink again, but this time no lever and no window. The rats were content for a little while but then started to 'misbehave' – chewing the walls, fighting with each other and rubbing their fur off. This led to a second conclusion: that intelligent creatures, such as rats and children, will do anything to stop themselves from being bored, including things that could be seen as silly or destructive.

But the experiment had still not finished! Next the researchers got nasty. The same rats were again put into another cage, again with food and drink, but this time with little wires placed across the floor and attached to a battery! (You need a twisted mind to be a child psychologist, obviously!) Every so often an electric current would be sent through the wires that would give the rats a mild shock.

Then came the finale of the experiment. The rats were taken out of the cages and given a choice of going back into any one of the three cages:

- Cage 1 – food, drink and a good film;
- Cage 2 – food and drink;
- Cage 3 – food, drink and being hooked up to a 12-volt car battery every few minutes.

Which did they choose? Well, not surprisingly Cage 1 was top of every rat's list. The twist, though, was that Cage 1 was then removed as an option and the rats were given a choice between Cage 2 and Cage 3. A 'no-brainer', you would have thought. But no, the surprising result here was that the rats went for Cage 3 next rather than Cage 2. This led to the final conclusion of the experiment – that intelligent creatures, such as rats and children, would rather have bad things happen than nothing at all.

When it comes to dealing with children, the obvious lesson from all this is that you need to give them attention. It may now be very clichéd, but spending 'quality time' with them is important. Children who don't get the attention that they need will then start to 'misbehave' in order to get it. Sometimes they know it is the only way to get it. It is a classic situation where children can be playing quietly and constructively and get totally ignored by their parents, but as soon as they start to fight and bicker they get told off. If this is an ongoing pattern, then the fights and bickering will start to happen on purpose if the children realise that this is the only way to get the attention they crave. I've seen it happen. It may be negative, 'painful' attention, but at least it's attention.

> EVERYBODY WANTS TO BE RECOGNISED AND SEEN AS WORTHWHILE.

An interesting time in most households with young children is teatime – it's the end of the day, everybody is tired, the house is in a mess and Johnny doesn't like carrots and is refusing to eat his tea. Again, the easy trap to fall into is to start getting cross with Johnny and getting into a big debate/confrontation/argument about his tea. Again, he's getting the attention he craves; even if it's not the best sort of attention, it's better than nothing. It's fascinating if you're able to stand back from the situation and instead focus attention and praise on the sibling who is eating his tea – after all, he's the one that is doing what you want him to do. After five or ten minutes or so of being ignored and deprived of the attention, it's amazing how quickly (usually) the errant child sees sense and complies. I've watched my own children in this situation go from screaming from behind the sofa that they won't eat their tea, to sheepishly crawling to the table saying that maybe they'll have a little bit, to sitting in their chair wolfing the lot and saying, 'Mummy, aren't I doing good tea eating?' – all without having one word spoken to them by their parents, who are busily lavishing attention on their brothers.

This fundamental need for attention, and doing whatever it takes to get it, doesn't disappear when we turn into adults. Sure, there are people who are real 'attention seekers' in a loud and extrovert way, and there are the shy, retiring types who don't want attention in such a 'sociable' way. But everybody still wants to be recognised and seen as worthwhile.

In *The Secret of Happy Children*, Steve Biddulph goes on to say,

> *We need to be recognised, noticed and, preferably, given sincere praise. We want to be included in conversations, have our ideas listened to and even admired.*

> *A three-year-old says it out straight: 'Hey, look at me.' Most of the adult world is made up of three-year-olds running about shouting, 'Look at me, Daddy.'*

The difference in adults is that they do not resort to negative attention in the way that children do. So I would not advise you to go round the office shouting at people, thinking that you are doing them a service by providing them with the attention that they need. However, the understanding that people need even a small bit of attention is a very useful one.

Praise

'Daddy, you're so clever!'

Jeremy, *Chitty Chitty Bang Bang* (1968)

HAVING just told you that you can motivate people, to a certain extent, by giving them any sort of attention, I want to tell you about one *particular* sort of attention that is the best. Praise.

Now I am a pretty secure and confident person. Not 100 per cent, but not bad. I get paid a perfectly decent salary and I like to think that I'm one of those people who are pretty self-motivated and put in a fair day's work for a fair day's pay, day in, day out. However, a while ago I had to organise and chair a series of meetings with a number of different suppliers we use. At each meeting, I got a bunch of the supplier's managers together with a bunch of our managers, with the aim of working out a plan for what the supplier needed to do to support Airbus's needs in the long term. It was all pretty routine stuff – I was just doing my job, though it was a bit of a slog. At the end of the week, we finished off the last meeting and I was at my desk tidying up ready to go home for the weekend. Just before I left, one of our team, who was also on her way home, came over to my desk. She said thanks for sorting the meetings out and that she thought they had gone really well and had been really useful. The conversation was over in less than a minute, and in the grand scheme of my career the meetings had been no big deal at all, but her comments made me feel fantastic. With under 60 seconds' worth of effort, she had ensured that, if she ever needed any work from me in the future, I would be more than happy to do the necessary to provide it.

Praise is an incredibly powerful motivator, if not the *most* powerful. What's more, providing it is dead easy and it's dirt-cheap.

In *The One Minute Manager*, Kenneth Blanchard and Spencer Johnson talk at length about the 'one-minute praising' and the fact that managers should try to catch people doing something right! Praising is put forward as a must for any successful manager. If you praise somebody as soon as they have done something well and make it clear what they have done well, then not only do they feel good about themselves, but they know exactly what you want from them and what they should be doing more of in the future.

A few warnings, though. First, praising isn't something that should be left for the annual appraisal and dished out once a year as token evidence of your compassionate side and to keep HR happy. It's an ongoing activity that is part of your everyday job. Second, praise has to be sincere. If the praise you are giving comes across as something you're doing because you read in some management book that it's a good idea, then nobody is going to feel very motivated. It has to be something that you really mean and is very genuine. Finally, the performance that is being praised has to be worthy of praise. Again, picking up on absolutely anything to praise is going to demotivate people rather than motivate them. You should be actively looking for performance to praise, should catch them doing something right – but don't cross the line and have people wondering why you are praising them for something that is routine or not even that good.

Praise is just as important for children. In fact, pretty much every book I have read on raising children, and every book I have read on management, agree that praise is crucial for developing capable, confident children and crucial for motivating your team at work.

In *The Sixty Minute Father*, Rob Parsons says that most of us know how effective praise can be at work but forget about it when it comes to our children. In my experience, though, it is generally the other way round. I do know there are parents, especially fathers, who have a pathological inability to praise their children, but generally I think that these days people are far more comfortable praising their children than they are at praising somebody they are managing at work.

The workplace is often still a male-dominated and macho place where the aim is to catch people doing something wrong, and praising, complimenting or saying thank you is seen as a bit 'wussy' and not a sign of strong management. But, given that praise is such a powerful motivator, this is an attitude that has to be quashed, and handing out praise, liberally, needs to be seen as the good thing that it is. I always find it amusing how much praise we lavish on babies when they take their first steps, or utter their first word – both things that, if

> PRAISE IS AN INCREDIBLY POWERFUL MOTIVATOR. WHAT'S MORE, PROVIDING IT IS DEAD EASY AND DIRT-CHEAP.

they didn't do, we would get really concerned about. Just imagine how powerful it would be if, as managers, we could give just a fraction of that praise to employees when they do things that are nowhere near as common.

Don't Grow Mushrooms

'When I was born I was so surprised I didn't talk for a year and a half.'

Gracie Allen, comedienne

ONE of the things that everybody hates is being kept in the dark – something that, unfortunately, managers are all too often very good at doing. Hence the term 'mushroom management'. When it comes to motivation, anything that can be done to avoid growing mushrooms is a good idea.

If people don't know what's going on, they become suspicious. They feel that they are being left out of the 'bigger picture', either on purpose or out of thoughtlessness, and they start to feel resentful, left out, rejected, undervalued and unimportant. They don't feel motivated to work towards the final goal, either because they don't know what it is (because nobody's told them), or they feel that there is some hidden agenda. In order to avoid this, a manager needs to be good at something that is talked about a lot on training courses (to the extent that it has become a cliché), but is less frequently put into practice. Communication.

There are a number of reasons why managers fail to communicate properly with their teams:

a   they don't feel that the information they have is important or interesting;
b   they think that the information they have is *too* important and interesting;
c   they haven't got the time;
d   they don't feel that people will understand the information;
e   it's just not their style.

However ...

a   What may not seem to be particularly important or interesting to you may actually be really useful to somebody in your team and could help them get something done more quickly or effectively.

b   Undoubtedly some information is confidential and can't be broadcast around the company, but a lot of information that managers think is too 'important' to share is actually quite safe to publish. It's more a case that the manager feels, maybe subconsciously, that holding onto certain information makes them seem more important. In any case, if you don't trust your team with important information, are you employing the right people in the first place?

c   Time must be made for communicating with your team. When it comes to the choice between a motivated team and a demotivated team, it is a 'no-brainer'.

d   Any manager who thinks that they are the only one clever enough to understand stuff is almost certainly wrong: people understand an awful lot more than is often immediately obvious. Steve Biddulph, writing in *The Secret of Happy Children*, tells an interesting story to illustrate this. The down-to-earth parents of abnormally intelligent children were asked what their secret was for raising such geniuses. Their trick, it turned out, was that they simply explained things to them. For example, while hoovering the house, carrying the baby on her back, the mother would explain that the noise was made by the vacuum cleaner's motor, which turned very fast because it was connected to electricity and that it blew lots of air. Twenty-one years later, the baby was doing doctoral research into spinal cell damage!

e   Make it your style

There are a number of ways to make sure your team are not turned into mushrooms and feel that they do know what is going on and are actually part of the team. The vehicle that is used is very much dependent upon the type and level of information that needs to be communicated, so a degree of judgement is important in determining which is most appropriate for the circumstances. All of the following, though, are up for grabs:

- one-to-one discussions
- formal reports
- regular operational team meetings
- quarterly company overview presentations
- newsletters
- intranet site
- display boards
- away days
- distribution of DVDs
- posters
- flyers
- town hall meetings
- video conferences
- emails.

There are probably more, but this list certainly demonstrates that there are plenty of ways of getting information to people, so there really is no excuse for not doing so. As a result, people will feel (I hope) not only that they have all the necessary information to do their day job properly but also that they understand what the bigger picture is and where they fit into it. They will also feel that they are valued members of a team, both at an operational level and a company level.

Communication, though, should not be a one-way process. Team members need to feel that they are being listened to and that they have an input into the topic of discussion or decisions that are being made, even if that input is not necessarily acted upon. It's like deciding where to go on the family holiday. If Dad arrives home one evening and calls the family together to announce that he has booked a fortnight in Siberia, bird spotting, then he is unlikely to get an enthusiastic response or enjoy his holiday. Everybody knows that it's just about impossible to book a holiday that is perfect for everybody, but, if you at least have the debate, all the family members feel they have had an input and that their views are valued, even if the final decision is not their dream holiday.

> IF PEOPLE
> DON'T KNOW
> WHAT'S GOING ON,
> THEY BECOME
> SUSPICIOUS.

At the end of the day, if people know what's going on and feel that they are being listened to, they are going to be far more motivated to put in a good day's work. If not, then you too will have fallen into the trap of mushroom management and all you get is an office full of perches for gnomes.

Get Out the Crayons

'All children are artists. The problem is how to remain an artist once he grows up.'

Pablo Picasso

WALK into any house that is home to young children and what can you guarantee you will find – apart from the toys strewn across the floor, *Thomas the Tank Engine* videos next to the TV and a well-used potty in the bathroom? Answer? Paintings. Not masterpieces by Renoir, Monet and Rolf Harris, but pictures of 'my house', 'Mummy, Daddy and the dog', 'a boat' and so forth by 'Bobby, aged 5' and 'Sally, aged 2'. Admittedly, you generally won't find them hanging above the mantelpiece in the newly decorated living room (though my parents did actually frame an awful painting of a bush I did when I was nine!) but you can pretty much guarantee that they will be on the fridge in the kitchen, or on a spare wall in the cloakroom. And are these paintings any good? No – they're terrible (sorry, kids). You couldn't flog them at a car-boot sale or sell them on eBay if you tried. You would struggle to pay people to take them away.

So why do parents do it? Motivation. It's our way of showing Bobby and Sally that we value what they do and are proud of their efforts and what they have produced. OK, it may not be a Renoir, but for them, and where they are in life, it might as well be. Seeing that their picture is good enough to go up on the wall gets them to say to themselves, 'Well, if that's good, then I'll do another one, but this time I'll paint the cat as well.'

Schools do exactly the same – in fact, parents would be concerned if they went to their kids' schools and found bare and drab walls. I don't know if teachers are told to do this at training college, but they probably don't need to be. As with parents, it's instinctive that displaying children's work, even as they get older, is a motivator. If you asked most parents why they do it, I'm sure they would have to think about it first, but I bet they would eventually find themselves giving an answer along these lines.

The other item that you will also increasingly find on the fridge door next to the paintings is a 'star chart'. The 'must-have' motivational technique of any modern-day child-rearing expert, the star chart can come in all sorts of configurations. The basic idea, though, is that a star (or any other shape with a self-adhesive backing) is awarded for any particular good behaviour that the parent wants to encourage, or for good behaviour in general. Actual rewards can be given when a certain number of stars has been reached – for example, sweets or a trip to the cinema. In a lot of respects, though, the important thing is that the star chart should be on view to display to everybody, and especially to the child in question, how 'good' the little darling has been.

In the workplace, too, there is a whole range of motivational 'eye candy' that can be displayed: organisation charts, team photos, the project plan, departmental objectives, production output against target, monthly scrap levels, sales targets, or any other key performance indicators – the list is endless.

Now, quite often, having this type of information on view is useful purely from a communications point of view, in that, if it's on the wall or a display board, then people will stand a better chance of seeing it and understanding the facts that are being shown. However, the real reason for displaying such information is the motivation it provides. If people see their name on a large org chart for all to see, they feel valued as employees and part of an important team. If they see that the sales figures are moving upwards, they feel driven to put in the effort to reach the annual target. Sure, we'll call it something like a 'visual management tool' or a 'head-up display' along with the appropriate three-letter acronym (VMT or HUD) to make it sound really clever, but make no mistake, this is just the same as the stuff on the fridge door.

There are two tricks that need to be remembered, though. First, keep it neat. Whatever is displayed should be done professionally. Tatty bits of paper don't make anybody feel valued. Second, keep it current. Data needs to be kept up to date and relevant. If not, then the display loses its credibility. Other than that, it's just a case of getting creative!

Incentives

> 'The only carrots that interest me are the number of carats in a diamond.'

Mae West

IN our house, there are metaphoric carrots lying all over the place. When it comes to motivating children, they are incredibly useful and incredibly common. I also know that it's not just our house that's full of them. All parents turn to them on a regular basis. 'Johnny, if you eat your vegetables you can have a sweetie after tea.' 'Polly, if you pass five GCSEs you can have that pony you've always wanted.'

Parents use them all the time. In a lot of respects they are a fallback solution. You're really taking advantage of the basic human desire to have more. If you're doing all the right things – such as praising when it's warranted – then, in theory, such blatantly exploitative measures shouldn't be necessary. But they do work. Very well. And, quite frankly, when you're visiting the grandparents and you've got three boys refusing to eat their lovingly prepared swede-and-spinach surprise (with a hint of Brussels sprout) then it's time to take whatever measures are necessary. It may be bribery, but it'll do me.

At work, the biggest 'carrot' that needs to be in place is salary. Very few of us turn up to work for charity. No matter how much somebody enjoys what they do, if they're not taking home enough money to pay the mortgage, pay the bills, feed and clothe the children, pay for the holiday and have enough left over for a pint of Guinness and a packet of salt-and-vinegar crisps every other Friday night, then they are not going to feel motivated. In fact, they're probably going to be spending far more time looking for a new job than they are producing anything worthwhile for you.

But carrots don't just have to be financially based. Far from it. There are plenty of other incentives available – company award ceremonies, dinners out, bottles of champagne, prizes for employee of the month, buying a bag of doughnuts. All of which can be used to motivate employees, often without your having to dig too deeply into the company's coffers.

By far the most novel incentive scheme I've ever come across was when I spent 6 months working in Mexico (it was a tough job, but somebody had to do it). I was working in a pretty large factory, two hours northwest of Mexico City, that produced drive shafts for large automotive manufacturers in Mexico – mainly Volkswagen and Chrysler. It was a relatively new factory, efficiently run, full of the latest manufacturing kit and surrounded by lawns, hedges and flower beds, despite temperatures in the 90s and basically being located in the middle of the desert. Quite the opposite of what you would expect of any factory in Mexico. They put the English automotive industry to shame.

One of the things the managing director of the company was very keen on was good housekeeping throughout the factory. And it showed. Whereas the equivalent UK factory would have floors covered in oil and grease, tools lying around, scrap parts lying around, swarf everywhere and Page 3 girls stuck to every available wall space, in Mexico you could eat your dinner off the floor, everything had a storage space allocated and the only page 3s around were those in the copies of the health-and-safety manual located around the plant for easy access by all employees.

And how did the MD achieve such standards? With the help of 'Miss Clean and Tidy'. Or, to use her correct title (if my very rusty Spanish serves me correctly) 'Señorita Limpia y Ordenada'. Basically, Miss Clean and Tidy was a leggy blonde model. And, believe me, leggy blonde models are in short supply in any part of

Mexico, let alone some outback in the desert that nobody has ever heard of. Each month, Miss Clean and Tidy would turn up at the plant to have her photo taken with the team who had won the Cleanest and Tidiest Production Line competition. And what was Miss Clean and Tidy wearing? A swimming costume and a sash!

The Mexicans loved it. For days beforehand, an almost audible buzz would go round the factory in anticipation of what this month's Miss Clean and Tidy would look like. It was a different leggy blonde each time, to make sure that interest was maintained. On the big day itself, the whole factory would assemble on the lush lawn outside to watch Miss Clean and Tidy present the winning team with a small prize and stand, in a classic model pose with one leg slightly bent, to have her photo taken with each team member in turn.

Now I would definitely not recommend this approach in the UK. You would be hauled up in front of the Equal Opportunities Commission in no time. But, by heck, did it work for a bunch of testosterone-filled Mexican blokes! A classic incentive scheme if ever there was one.

Incentive schemes are something that any manager can implement, even if it's on the smallest scale. Anybody can arrange for a crate of beer for the team producing the best design, for example. Even if the cost comes out of your own pocket, it may be worth it for the effect that it can have. Schemes do need to be appropriate, which requires some judgement on the manager's part: too stingy and they can lose credibility and become a joke; too over the top and they can be seen as unfair by those who miss out on the prize. However, used cleverly, they can be a good way of reaching really high levels of motivation.

Fun

'In every task that must be done, there is an element of fun.'

Mary Poppins, *Mary Poppins* (1964)

ONE of the big decisions Melanie and I made as parents happened when Jack reached the age of three: it was time to send him to nursery school. We were quite fortunate in that where we live there are a plethora of nursery schools. The place is full of them. We therefore spent quite some time looking through brochures and visiting various establishments that we had heard were worth a try.

After much deliberation we made our selection. We chose the 'successful' establishment on the basis that they had quite a rigid structure to the day and quite a formal method for 'teaching' the children. Don't get me wrong, it wasn't some sort of boot camp for the under-fives – there were all the toys, sandpits and paintings you would expect to see in any nursery. But it was definitely run more along the lines of a school than most of the places we looked at. Our logic at the time was that Jack would benefit from the structure and that it would be good preparation for when he moved on to school for real.

Now, you can see this one coming, I'm sure, but, after Jack started at the nursery, it soon became apparent that he wasn't very happy. At first we put it down to his getting used to being away from his mum and being in a strange place. However, after a couple of months, he was still crying when he was dropped off – we could tell that he wasn't settling in. The look of relief when he saw that one of us had arrived to pick him up said it all. After much deliberation, we decided that enough was enough and that we should look at moving him to a different nursery.

Having learned from our original mistake, this time we went for somewhere that was far more relaxed and where the focus was much more on having fun. The difference was amazing. After only a couple of days at the new nursery, he stopped crying. It wasn't long before it started to become difficult to get Jack to leave at the end of a session and, when we asked him what he had been doing during the day, we would get an excited list of activities rather than just a grunt and 'I can't remember', as we used to. It was a huge relief to us. It had been torture, especially for Melanie, to see Jack so unhappy at the old place, but it was also difficult to know whether we were making the right decision to move him. Were we being premature? Should we give him longer to settle in? Were we just disrupting him by moving him? Fortunately, our decision was vindicated.

> PEOPLE WHO ARE HAVING FUN AT WORK ARE MORE SWITCHED ON, THINK BETTER AND ARE MORE PRODUCTIVE.

The whole episode highlighted to us just how important it is for kids to have fun. When they're babies, all we do with them is try to have fun. The first smile is always a major event that is communicated to family and friends in a major newsflash. After that, all manner of funny faces are pulled to get the child to repeat the feat as often as possible. However, the older children get, the more fun is given a back seat and they are told that they need to get down to the serious business of learning, education and growing up.

Having fun with kids, though, is really important – not only does it make them happy, rounded people, but it actually helps them to learn. Apparently, chemical changes in the brain during positive emotions have beneficial effects on brain growth. Jack learned far more quickly at the nursery he was having fun at than he did at the one that in theory was teaching him more. Now that he has started at 'big' school, he gets given a 'maths game' each week to bring home. This is basically a simple board game that has some sort of mathematical lesson behind it. He loves playing them and begs me to play with him when he brings a new one home. He has no idea that as well as having fun he's also starting to learn to add and subtract.

However, once the process of making life serious does begin, there is no stopping it. School, good manners, exams, respecting your elders, more exams, driving test, more exams. By the time we get to our first job, any sense of fun has been well and truly drummed out of us. Any that is left is certainly not something you bring to work with you.

Yet having fun at work, and even 'playing', is a constructive thing to do. Just as children learn more by having fun, people who are having fun and are happy at work are more switched on, think better and are more productive. Obviously there's a job to be done and you can't be 'having a laugh' the whole time; but, likewise, if the culture that a manager creates is one in which only work, work, work is acceptable and anyone seen smiling is obviously not working hard enough, then they're not going to get the best from their team.

Now it's very easy to say that it's good to have fun at work – very convenient. 'Where's the science?' I hear you cry. Well, my evidence comes from that well-known and highly respected academic journal – the KLM in-flight magazine, *Holland Herald* (July 2004 issue, to be precise)! It was while passing the time on a long-haul flight out of Amsterdam that I read an article by Jane

Szita under the heading 'I Play, Therefore I Am'. In it she described how, through play, we relieve stress, discharge emotions, learn new skills and find satisfaction and enjoyment. Children play to develop socially, emotionally and intellectually – indeed, to survive. This is why more intelligent mammals, such as dolphins, continue to play into adulthood. Apparently, during play, people reach a heightened state of 'flow' relating to alpha brainwaves, which have been recorded in people who play computer games, top sportsmen and Buddhist monks. Jane Szita argues that our current Dickensian work ethic should therefore be replaced by a play ethic, whereby people operate in this a state of 'flow'.

Now I don't know about your office, but in mine the introduction of a play ethic is probably some way off. However, I do like the idea of people's minds getting into a state of 'flow' because they see work as play. The conclusion that I draw is that if you can make work fun, at least just a little bit, then you can get some alpha brainwaves going and reap some of the benefits talked about in the article – learning new skills, providing the brain with a workout, heightening awareness.

When I worked in management consultancy, one of the best-known events in the firm was 'Third Friday'. Basically, because the vast majority of people within the firm were scattered around the country and abroad, working for clients, developing any sense of community in the firm was quite difficult. If you were working at a client's premises for a long time, you often felt that you were more a member of their company than your own.

In order to address this, every third Friday of the month would be set aside for everybody in the firm to return to the office in London. There was no set format for the day – there could, for instance, be meetings for various functional groups within the firm, presentations on topics of current business interest, training sessions and one-to-one meetings with managers or mentors. The only regular event was at the end of the day. Everybody, including the partners of the firm, would decamp to a nearby bar for drinks while partaking in the customary pub quiz. While some of the stuff was quite serious, generally the atmosphere of the day was quite relaxed and the emphasis was certainly more on having fun than grinding out a hard day's work – there was plenty of time for that during the rest of the month.

There's no way you could prove that this bit of 'fun' was of any benefit to the firm. In fact, these Third Fridays cost the firm a significant amount of money in lost revenue. When you bill your clients by the hour, and most people are being charged out at over £100 per hour, some significantly more, keeping an office of a few hundred consultants away from the client for a day is no small decision. However, the partners of the firm knew that what they lost in revenue on that day, they made up for during the rest of the month because they had a team of motivated people who went away from the event feeling that they worked for a firm that valued fun, even if it could be another month before they set foot in its office again. The benefit may have been difficult to measure objectively, but subjectively they knew it was the right thing to do.

Exactly how you bring some frivolity to your team depends on the company, the people, the type of work and what is appropriate. What's clear, though, is that there is no longer any need to feel guilty about turning up at the office and having a bit of fun!

PERFORMANCE

'The first rule of leadership: everything is your fault.'

Hopper, *A Bug's Life* (1998)

A few weeks after being made a manager, I came to a realisation. The thunderbolt that hit me was how totally dependent my own performance was on the performance of my team. I could achieve nothing, and impress nobody, unless my team worked conscientiously and efficiently to produce the results that were required of them, which in turn were the results that were being asked of me by my lords and masters in the organisation. Each time I reported my project's progress and status to my own manager, it was other people's work I was reporting on, not my own.

It was really quite an earth-shattering realisation for me. Here I was, having spent years in full-time education revising fervently each summer to make sure I passed the latest round of exams, and the first years of my career meticulously carrying out the requested calculations or writing the critical report, confronted by the scary prospect that it was no longer just a matter of how hard *I* worked, or how many hours *I* put in. No, if my team didn't perform and produce the goods, I was done for.

I began to realise just how the football coach on the touchline feels each Saturday afternoon. Yes, he can flap his arms around furiously and shout instructions at people (politely, of course); and, yes, he can make a few strategic substitutions. But, on the whole, the coach is totally dependent on how each player in the team performs on the day. The result is, to a certain extent, out of his hands. If the players do well, he gets to lift the silverware. If they do badly, for whatever reason, he is asked to spend more time with his family (a fate worse than death!).

I had a similar realisation when Jack started going to school. On his first day, just a few hours after trotting off in his new school uniform, looking as angelic as is possible for one of my offspring, Jack trotted home again at the end of the day to tell us that he had been in trouble with the dinner ladies! Now when your four-year-old comes home with such devastating news all sorts of things run through your mind. Is he already the school troublemaker? Will the authorities be round to interview me? Will he get a record? Is this the beginning of the slippery slope to Borstal, youth detention centre, prison?

After being subjected to a thorough interrogation by his two concerned parents, Jack revealed that he had launched a rubber quoit he had been given to play with at lunchtime into the air and that it had come back down to rest on the school roof. He had then been told off for his heinous crime by one of the dinner ladies, muttering something about having to get the caretaker out, and then frogmarched to his new teacher for the severity of his actions to be reinforced! Fortunately, time has shown (so far) that Jack hasn't turned out to be a troublemaker, and Borstal seems less likely these days, but the whole incident, amusing as it was, did demonstrate to me and Melanie that our son's actions were no longer completely within our control. He had been released into the big wide world and what he got up to while we were not there was now up to him, but would still very much reflect on us. It was a daunting prospect.

Fortunately, be you football coach, parent or manager, you are not completely at the mercy of your squad, children or team. There are things that you can do. You may not be able to do the actual work itself, but you can establish the right environment for people to work in. Everything needs to put in place to enable everybody in your team to reach their full potential.

Setting Goals and Objectives

'Do, or do not. There is no try.'

Yoda, *The Empire Strikes Back* (1980)

PERHAPS the most important thing to do in order to get people to perform at their maximum potential is to set them goals or objectives (I do know people who define these two terms differently, but as far as I'm concerned they are the same thing). If people do not know what you want them to do, then they can hardly be expected to do it well. Setting objectives makes it clear what you expect of people, helps them to prioritise when the day-to-day workload starts to mount up and gives people something to aim for. Otherwise, it's very easy for people to turn up to the office each day, put in a good eight hours of 'work' and achieve nothing in particular. Setting goals and objectives is one of the most powerful tools a manager has.

There is a train of thought – which is a particularly British trait (of which I am reminded each summer when I watch the tennis at Wimbledon) – that, as long as you try your best, that is good enough. This is admirable but (as is proved by the number of recent British Wimbledon champions) pointless. The good thing about setting objectives is that it focuses on the achievement, not on how you get there. While putting on a 'good show' and coming a respectable second may be acceptable for some, objectives drive people to 'win'. In *The Truth About Managing People*, Stephen P. Robbins says,

> There is a mountain of evidence that tells us that people perform best when they have goals. More to the point, we can say that specific goals increase performance; that difficult goals, when accepted, result in higher performance than do

easy goals; and that feedback leads to higher performance than does nonfeedback.

Specific hard goals produce a higher level of output than does the generalized goal of 'do your best.' It's the specificity of the goal itself that acts as an internal stimulus. Goals tell employees what needs to be done and how much effort they'll need to expend to achieve it.

These days there are few commercial organisations that don't have some sort of objective-setting exercise included as part of their routine management process. Even outside industry, this is more and more the case.

I will always remember the first parents' evening I went to at the nursery school Jack attended. I was very excited at being so grown up now that I had to attend parents' evenings. After years of being left with the babysitter, as my own parents disappeared for their annual date with my delightful teachers, here I was, finally, in the position of power! OK, Jack was only three, but I couldn't wait to get home with a stern look on my face and keep him guessing over whether I was happy with his marks (all right, then, standard of hand painting).

> IF PEOPLE DO NOT KNOW WHAT YOU WANT THEM TO DO, THEN THEY CAN HARDLY BE EXPECTED TO DO IT WELL.

When we got to the nursery school we were shown photos of the various activities the children had been doing throughout the year – playing with water, playing in the sandpit, running around in the garden, making things out of Play-Doh, playing with the train set – all the usual stuff you would expect to see a bunch of kids who were knee high to a grasshopper doing. We were then shown all the paintings hanging up that had been produced by the collection of budding Picassos and the various bits of 'craft' that they had created. It was all very much as you would expect, and, unfortunately, not a mention of having trouble with quadratic equations or problems translating Latin that I could go home and have words with Jack over!

Just before we were about to leave, though, Jack's teacher came over to show us his 'booklet'. I have to admit that I was pretty surprised when we found it to contain numerous pages full of developmental targets. I felt compelled to tell the teacher that all that stuff about quadratic equations was just a joke! Apparently, though, the children's progress had to be recorded against national curriculum targets for their age. The targets were pretty basic – be able to wash own hands, be able to communicate with other children, be able to recognise different numbers, etc. But they were targets nonetheless. The children each had their own little colourful book with specific things they were going to do in the following few weeks in order to meet the appropriate targets. Here they were, at age three, already being set objectives!

Fortunately, the nursery-school staff were very pragmatic and didn't get hung up on them or let them get in the way, and, to be honest, the process was as much for the teachers as it was for the children. However, it clearly illustrated just how important objective setting has become across all walks of life. There's a reason for that: it works.

Imagine

'Imagine, imagine, imagine a story.'

Jelly and Jackson, *The Story Makers* (CBeebies TV)

THE human mind is an amazing thing. If you imagine something, you gravitate towards what you are imagining. So, for example, if you say to yourself that you mustn't forget to feed the cat, you end up forgetting to feed the cat. If you get a new car and drive around cautiously saying to yourself that you mustn't scratch it, you end up driving it into a brick wall.

I was on a training course once where this phenomenon was being discussed. There were over 100 people in the room and everybody was asked to close their eyes and to imagine biting into a lemon. We were told to concentrate hard on the picture of the lemon and focus on the juice in our mouths. Around the room, people started to giggle as they realised they were really starting to taste the lemon and get an unpleasant sensation on their taste buds. Weird.

> GET PEOPLE TO PICTURE THEMSELVES HAVING ACHIEVED THE OBJECTIVE. IT WILL HELP THEM TO ACHIEVE IT IN REALITY.

Apparently, this is all something to do with the fact that the mind works in pictures and can move only *towards* things, not away from them. So, if somebody says to you, 'Don't think about an orange penguin wearing pyjamas,' what do you think about? The penguin in his pyjamas. We automatically gravitate to what's is in our minds.

This is a classic trap that parents fall into with their children. If a child is carrying a glass of blackcurrant juice across your mother-in-law's new, white, shag-pile carpet and you shout out, 'Johnny, be careful, don't you dare spill any of that juice!' you can pretty much guarantee what will happen. The picture of spilling the juice has been implanted in the child's mind and – lo and behold! – Granny's carpet gets ruined. It's very easy for parents to focus on the negative when talking to their children: *don't* break the delicate ornament, *don't* get your clothes dirty, *don't* lose your new pencil case, *don't* fall out of that tree – and so on.

The advice to parents is to change the way they speak to children so that the wording is positive, rather than negative: 'Johnny, make sure you walk carefully with that glass'; 'Hold the delicate ornament gently'; 'Keep your clothes clean'; 'Look after your new pencil case'; 'Hold onto those branches tightly.' This way, the kids are helped to think and act positively and to feel capable because they are being told what to do, not being frightened by being told what not to do.

The trick with goals and objectives, therefore, is to get people to imagine them. In *How To Be a Complete and Utter Failure in Life, Work and Everything*, Steve McDermott talks about the power of imagining desired outcomes and provides some tantalising proof that it works:

> Now it may sound like a couch potato's dream, but recent research has proven that you can even think yourself strong with imaginary exercises. Researchers asked ten volunteers aged 20 to 35 to imagine flexing one of their biceps as hard as possible in training sessions five times a week. The researchers, whose findings were reported in the magazine New Scientist, recorded the electrical brain activity during the sessions. To make sure volunteers were not unintentionally tensing and

moving their arms, they also monitored electrical impulses of their arm muscles. Every two weeks muscle strength was measured. The volunteers who thought about exercise showed a 13.5% increase and maintained that gain for three months after the training stopped.

Now *there's* something to go and try!

This technique of getting people to imagine the objective and what things will feel like once the objective has been achieved can be really powerful. I accept that if you ask your team to sit in a room together, close their eyes and imagine pictures of the annual sales target being achieved, then they will probably all think that you are stark raving bonkers and call in the men in white coats! But there are more subtle ways. For example, you can drop into a conversation with somebody that it'll be 'great to see this widget when we've finished building it', or you can put pictures on the wall of previous successes. Basically, anything you can do to get people to picture themselves having achieved the objective, the more chance you've got of getting them to achieve it in reality.

In fact, I used this technique myself as I wrote this book. Why? Well, to be perfectly frank with you, I've never written a book before. I therefore had no idea whether this whole writing-a-book thing was going to work out or not. If you don't mind my saying, it took up rather a lot of my time – something that's in short supply when you've got three kids to bring up, a job to hold down and a decorating project that is way, way behind schedule. At the end of it all, I could quite easily have ended up with pages of rambling nonsense of no use to anybody.

In order to try to avoid this outcome, therefore, I imagined what it would be like to be published – I tried to visualise what the book would look like and what it would be like to go into Waterstone's and see it on the shelf. OK, a bit mad. But what it did was make the outcome seem real and something that became almost a destiny. Not in any spiritual sense, but it did give the seemingly endless evenings (I must learn to type with more than two fingers someday) a focus and a tangible end result. Use your imagination. It does work.

Let People Make Lots of Mistakes

'Daddy, have you ever seen a volcano interrupting?'

Jack Durston

WATCHING a baby learn to walk is fascinating. Will is currently in the process of taking his first steps. He's not able to walk on his own yet, but is starting to give the paintwork on my recently painted skirting boards a run for its money with his baby-walking trolley. He pushes it across the room at great speed, in a process more accurately described as perpetual stumbling than walking, and then comes to an abrupt halt as he smashes into the wall on the other side of the room.

It took Will a while to get this far, though. The first time he used the baby walker he held on tight with a slightly bemused look on his face. As the little trolley slowly started to move, he kept his feet firmly planted to the spot, and slowly fell face first to the ground as the trolley moved further away! That's my boy! He's since come a cropper in all manner of ways – falling forwards, falling backwards, doing the splits, tripping up.

You would have thought that by now Will would have decided that this walking lark was a bit of a pain, and that it was best to give the whole thing up. 'All this banging me head – I think I'll stick with that crawling business. Much safer.' But no. In fact you should see his reaction when you try to take the baby walker away after he's spent the past half-hour terrorising the household and doing his best to get himself a trip to A&E. He goes bonkers. He hates to stop, despite the steadily growing collection of bruises. There's absolutely no getting in his way. He could go on for hours.

Also, Sam loves doing jigsaws and has always been able to finish those that are aimed at kids above his age group. His technique, as well as being pretty observant and good with pictures, is to try each piece, rotate it by 90 degrees, and if it doesn't fit try it again, then rotate it by 90 degrees, if it doesn't fit, repeat again, try another piece, and so on. It can be a bit painstaking, but it works, and his face when he finishes is always worth it!

It's interesting how this trial-and-error method is seen as perfectly normal and acceptable for babies and young children, but the older we get, the more it is frowned upon until, by the time we get to work, the idea of making a mistake or 'failing' has become abhorrent. How many people have said, as their teenage children go out into the world armed with hormones and acne cream, 'Well, you've got to let them make their own mistakes'? Even when kids are that age, parents reluctantly acknowledge that making mistakes is a necessary learning experience.

However, once at work, togged up in our suits and ties, we're all expected to be very clever people, to be perfect and to get everything right first time. Everybody treads cautiously and takes as few risks as possible in order to avoid the humiliation of 'getting something wrong'. Well, if you want to get your team to perform well, then this is a way of thinking that you have to discourage and avoid. People need to understand that, if they make mistakes or things don't work out, they will not be criticised or 'punished'. Mistakes need to be seen as something to be learned from.

When I say mistakes, I don't mean things that could be avoided by being more accurate or careful. This is not a *carte blanche* for poor quality and sloppiness. What I do mean is that, when an approach to a problem has been taken that is new and contains an element of calculated risk, but did not work out, then people should not be hauled over the coals for having failed. Instead, they should be encouraged to take risks, learn from the experience when things don't work out and apply the learning next time. It is no coincidence that successful entrepreneurs like Branson, Gates and Sugar are also risk takers (as Branson likes to demonstrate by doing something silly in a hot-air balloon every other year).

At the beginning of this book I talked about when I was first made a manager and had to get some parts manufactured as part of a product-development programme. I made a number of mistakes at the time – getting something new made on a night shift, promising delivery of the parts before I knew they were correct. My boss at the time could easily have come down on me like a ton of bricks and brought an early end to my managerial career. Fortunately, he was more constructive

> PEOPLE SHOULD BE ENCOURAGED TO TAKE RISKS, LEARN FROM EXPERIENCE WHEN THINGS DON'T WORK OUT AND APPLY THEIR LEARNING THE NEXT TIME.

than that, and I was able to learn from the experience and take away some valuable lessons: believe me, I've never asked for any prototyping work to be done on a night shift since. These days, with my own team, if and when things do go wrong, rather than carry out a witch hunt, I always try to give people the opportunity to analyse what happened and determine what they can do to ensure that it doesn't happen again.

Failure, if that is the right word, should be seen as a positive thing, not a negative one, and should almost be encouraged (within reason!). Soichiro Honda, the founder of Honda Motor Company, said, 'Success can only be achieved through repeated failure and introspection. In fact, success represents 1 per cent of your work, which results only from the 99 per cent that is called failure.'

Unfortunately, mistakes are usually seen as a problem, and most people don't recognise the positive side of 'failure'. However, successful people and teams see mistakes as feedback on how they are doing. You learn far more when things go wrong because people contemplate, analyse, regroup and develop an alternative approach. When things go well, we just say great and go onto the next thing. Successful people and teams actually make far more mistakes than the unsuccessful ones who can become paralysed by their fear of failure. They may make more mistakes in the process of getting there, but the end result is much greater than it would have been without them.

History is littered with people who went through periods of 'failure' before achieving success. Henry Ford's first businesses went bankrupt, Edison developed thousands of light bulbs before finding one that worked and Werner von Braun tested thousands of rockets before inventing the V2 and Saturn V. Abraham Lincoln failed in business aged 22, lost a legislative race at 23, again failed in business at 25, had a nervous breakdown when he was 27, lost Congressional races aged 34, 37 and 39, lost a senatorial race aged 46, failed to be elected as vice-president aged 47 and lost another senatorial contest at 49. At 52, he was finally elected president. Most of us would have packed up and gone home, tired, aged 51! Lincoln, like the baby learning to walk, just kept on getting up again and giving it another try.

Questions, Questions, Questions

'Knowing the answers means asking the right questions.
Finding the right questions is the art of management.'

Mike Woods, *The Manager's Casebook*

VERY much linked with the fear of failure is the fear of looking stupid. Again, in the work environment there is an unwritten rule that everybody has to appear very clever and that they know everything, or nearly everything. As a result, another skill that children are masters of is suppressed – the art of asking questions.

Anybody with young children will know just what experts they are at questioning their parents to the point of exasperation. For some reason they seem to enjoy doing it right up until their lives are being put in real danger!

SAM: Daddy, why are you sitting in that seat?

DADDY: Because I'm driving the car, son.

SAM: Why don't you sit in the other seat?

DADDY: Because this one's got the steering wheel in front of it.

SAM: Why has that one got the steering wheel in front of it?

DADDY: Because it has.

SAM: Why has it?

DADDY: Because the steering wheel's always on this side of the car.

SAM: Why is the steering wheel on that side of the car?

DADDY: Because in Britain we drive on the left-hand side of the road.

SAM: Why do we drive on the left-hand side of the road, and who's Britain?

DADDY: Because we do.

SAM: Why do we?

DADDY: Because somebody decided to.

SAM: Who decided to?

DADDY: I have no idea. Now be quiet.
SAM: Daddy?
(Pause)
SAM: How much further?

However, the older we get, the less curious we seem to be, as if the ability to ask questions had been drilled out of us. However, when you're managing a team, being able to ask the right questions is critical in order to determine whether or not they are progressing along the track you have set them, or whether they need to go in a different direction.

One of the best bosses I have worked for had a fantastic ability to ask the right questions. I was a consultant, and since I was at the client's site most of the time I would go for quite long periods without seeing him. The work I was doing was quite complicated and I was having to work in a very sensitive and political environment. There was also no formal, written reporting between us. However, when he did come and visit me, within 20 minutes of our sitting down he would have a complete grasp of the intricacies of the project, where things were up to and what was the best way forward, all through asking the right questions. He always seemed to know exactly what to ask, and if, for some very strange reason, I didn't give a satisfactory answer, he knew how to drill further and push me until he got the answer he needed. He was so good at asking questions that he actually got me coming up with my own actions during the meeting. There was no need to ask me to do anything because it was obvious from my answers that there was something missing or that something needed doing. All this was done in a very pleasant, but firm manner. It was a grilling, but you didn't realise it until it was all over.

What was also interesting was that he would have no hesitation in leading into a question with, 'I'm probably being a bit slow here' or, 'I don't understand this, so help me.' Now this was a highly intelligent guy, very senior in the firm, and probably earning more than you or I could ever dream of. And yet he had no problem admitting when he was unsure of something or had gaps in his knowledge or understanding. What he did make certain of, though, was that, by asking pertinent questions, he had filled those gaps by the time he had finished with me.

> BEING SCARED OF ASKING A QUESTION, NO MATTER HOW STUPID YOU THINK IT MIGHT BE, IS THE WORST MISTAKE YOU CAN MAKE.

If you don't ask the right questions of your team, your understanding of what they have achieved, what they are doing and where they are going will be flawed. Being scared of asking a question, no matter how stupid you think it might be, is the worst mistake you can make. Practising asking lots of questions, and drilling beyond the initial superficial answer, will mean your understanding and knowledge of your team's performance will progress far more quickly. You will then be in a much stronger position to be able to take some positive action if necessary. If you are stumbling around in the dark, you won't.

Poor Performance

'Never fail to reward merit, but never let a fault go
unremarked.'

Seisei Kato, Toyota

OF course, by asking questions, you may well discover that things
are not going quite as you would like, or, more importantly, that
things are not going well because somebody is not pulling their
weight or not carrying out their work to a standard that could be
reasonably expected of them. I have already discussed the concept
of boundaries and how people test them. Well, poor performance
is another area where your boundaries are always being tested. If
people know that they are not pulling their weight, but you're not
picking up on it, then they'll carry on performing (or not
performing) at that level.

I once had a guy in my team whose absenteeism started to become
a concern to me. He was not away for long periods of time, just
isolated days here and there, but it was happening frequently, and
often at really inconvenient points during the project. As time went
by, the excuses became more and more bizarre too. When he told
me that he had not come in one day because his wife had
discovered their neighbour, dead, in his garage, I decided enough
was enough! Now for all I know he may have been telling the
truth, but, whether he was or he wasn't, his performance was
suffering badly. I took him to one side and told him so, and that
his absences, justified or not, had to be reduced. We talked about
what we could both do to help him do this. It was an
uncomfortable conversation, but I felt better after it and the
situation definitely improved thereafter.

When you notice, therefore, that somebody, or a group of
people for that matter, is not performing, you can't just let it

go and keep your fingers crossed that things will get better. You need to be honest about the situation and address it. Otherwise, the team member becomes confused about what is acceptable performance and what is not, and you just become bitter. It is also going to reflect badly on your own performance. Carrying on regardless with your head in the sand, pretending everything is OK and that you are perfectly happy, is the worst thing you can do. In the way that children need to be 'disciplined' when they have misbehaved, it is really important that the person knows that you are unhappy with their work and that you actively inform them of this and that you expect something different from them. The two approaches are actually surprisingly similar, though I wouldn't suggest that you start telling your employees that they have been a very naughty boy and get them to stand in the corner with their hands on their head! There are steps to go through, though, that are common to both:

> WHEN DEALING WITH POOR PERFORMANCE, ADDRESS THE BEHAVIOUR, NOT THE PERSON. DISCIPLINING IS AT ITS WORST WHEN IT IS EMOTIONAL.

If children misbehave, we tell them off straightaway. We don't save up all of their misdemeanours during the course of a week and sit them down on a Sunday evening and shout at them (OK, talk firmly) for each one in turn. We know that they will have no idea what we are going on about and will have completely forgotten what it was they were doing at the time. You could pretty much guarantee, therefore, that they would go and do the same thing again the following week.

Similarly, as soon as you've decided that somebody's performance at work isn't acceptable, the first thing you need to do is inform them straightaway. It's no use waiting until things are a bit quieter or until the next performance review, not least because the performance could have had a seriously detrimental effect on your business by then. Also, the employee will not associate the poor performance with what they were doing at the time and will have lost an opportunity to learn from your feedback and make improvements.

Next, you need to tell them exactly what it is you have an issue with and how it makes you feel. This way, they can use the information to take steps to address the problem and improve their performance. If they know that their actions have consequences, making you disappointed, frustrated and angry, the desire to make improvements will be greater. When disciplining children, if you tell them that what they have done has made you sad, or their brother upset, for example, then it helps them to understand why their actions are unacceptable and why they are being told off. Otherwise they find it difficult to understand why they shouldn't poke their brother in the eye again. 'But it didn't hurt me.'

A crucial and often ignored point when dealing with poor performance is that it should be the behaviour or action that should be 'addressed', not the person. It is the same when disciplining children. You don't tell them that they have been naughty: you tell them that *what they have done* is naughty. Early in my career, I was in a meeting where a manager was not at all happy with the work that one group of people within a team had carried out. Things came to a head in this meeting and the manager confronted them over what they had been doing and how the work that they had produced was not what he was expecting – to put it politely. However, as the discussion progressed and became more heated, he questioned why they were needed at all and what use any of their work was in general, not just in this specific situation.

It was like a red rag to a bull. People's mindsets instantly went from the logical and the scientific to the personal and emotional. What was already a heated discussion went to a different level with a couple of short sentences. Moving from criticising the performance to criticising the people themselves changed the whole situation from a constructive one to a very destructive one. From then on, that particular group never truly worked as part of the team again.

Finally, finish by telling the person that you value what they do and their contribution to the team. This isn't to give the impression that the problem was not really a problem at all, but is to make sure that the person is motivated to address the problem and to reaffirm that it is the performance that is the issue, not the person.

Above all, make sure that you are consistent – if another person performs poorly in the same way, don't let it go unchallenged. Or, if the same person continues to perform poorly, don't ignore it.

One final step that I would add is that you need to try to understand what caused the poor performance in the first place. There can be a whole host of reasons: the person's objectives were not clear, they did not have the right training for the job, they were not clear on priorities, factors outside their control were involved, they have personal problems at home, etc. The list goes on. There needs to be some dialogue to get to the bottom of the cause and to determine what action you, or they, need to take to rectify the matter.

One of the things I have realised since having children is that good disciplining is actually all a bit of an act. In fact disciplining is at its worst when it is emotional and out of control. There are times when I've had to hold back the giggles while acting cross, because what has happened, while wrong, was actually quite amusing. I look back now at some of the times when I was told off by my own parents and realise that there were probably plenty of times when they went away afterwards and had a good laugh about it (and probably plenty of times when they didn't). It's the same when addressing poor performance with your team. All too often, such situations are seen as emotional and negative, when parties on both sides lose control. If you can successfully take the emotion away, though, and follow the steps above, what is ordinarily seen as a negative situation to be avoided at all costs can be turned into a positive situation that leads to improved performance.

From a parenting perspective, Dr Christopher Green puts it nicely in *New Toddler Taming*:

> *When the word* discipline *is used, many parents become flustered because they associate it with punishment, but this is not what it is all about. The word* discipline *has a Latin origin, which means teaching or training. The similar sounding word* disciple *comes from the Latin for 'a learner'. Discipline is a far more attractive concept when viewed as a learning experience for our children rather than one of pain and punishment.*

But this should equally apply in the workplace.

Conflict

'The ultimate measure of a man is not where he stands in moments of comfort and convenience, but where he stands at times of challenge and controversy.'

Martin Luther King Jr

CHALLENGING negative performance within your team means that a willingness to deal with conflict is important in any manager. Conflict is a day-to-day part of being a manager, and actually needs to be an integral part of a team in order that good decisions are made and overall performance raised. Conflict actually leads to better performance, something that to a lot of people is very counterintuitive.

In *Leadership and the Quest for Integrity*, Joseph L. Badaracco Jr and Richard R. Ellsworth say that:

> *Open and frank exchanges of ideas are essential to sound decision making and corporate morale. But openness and candor require that conflict be tolerated, even encouraged. As long as discussions are substantive – not driven by personal or subunit agendas – and as long as the discussions pre-suppose agreement with the leader's vision, disagreement and conflict are healthy. Such discussions can help develop wider ranges of alternatives and a better understanding of the strengths and weaknesses of each alternative.*

So there you go: having a damned good set-to is actually very healthy. If conflict is something you feel uneasy with, as did I for a long time, it's something that you need to learn to deal with. As I said earlier, the thing that changed my own approach to conflict was learning that everybody had a right to their view and a right to air that view – a concept that I found really powerful to help me continue driving with a controversial point, when in the past I would have given in and shut up much earlier. I now find that I deal with conflict on pretty much a daily basis and no longer come out the other side feeling as if I'd been through the mill.

However, conflict does bring with it another concept that can be very difficult for a lot of people to swallow: the fact that there are going to be people who dislike you. No matter how great a leader you are, how good you are at motivating people and how much you respect and value people, there are going to be times, in order to deliver the performance that you want, when you will have to make some difficult decisions.

> CONFLICT CAN ACTUALLY LEAD TO BETTER PERFORMANCE.

And difficult decisions, almost by definition, mean that somebody is not going to be happy with the outcome. Badaracco and Ellsworth are quite right in saying that conflict is constructive in the right environment and when everybody understands that conflict can be healthy. But, unfortunately, there are plenty of people around who do get upset when they are on the losing end of a confrontation and there are plenty of people around who get upset by management decisions generally.

Accepting that you cannot be everybody's 'friend' is an important step for a manager. This is especially the case for new managers, since they quite often find themselves managing the people they were previously mates with and with whom they spent lots of time criticising the old manager. In this situation, it's important to realise that you can no longer be 'one of the boys'. At the end of the day, being a manager does make you different.

Similarly, if, as a parent, you think that you are going to be appreciated and adored on a daily basis, then you've got something else coming. Raising children, from toddler to teenager, is one long conflict. All that changes is what the conflict is about: 'Mummy, can I have a new Thomas the Tank Engine?' to 'Mum, can I sleep over at my girlfriend's house?' Parents are constantly having to make decisions that they believe are right for their children but, more often than not, do not go down all that well with them. However, being firm and not giving in when the decision is greeted with a tantrum, be it at two or sixteen years old, is really important if any credibility is to be maintained. As they say, you have to be cruel to be kind. As a result, there can't be many parents who have not had various unpleasantries shouted at them at some point by their children.

Managers must recognise that, if they're going to run effective teams, then trying to be everybody's friend is going to get them nowhere.

Training is an Investment

'Kids are great. They practically raise themselves nowadays, you know, with the Internet and all.'

Homer Simpson, *The Simpsons*

IT'S obvious, isn't it? If you want somebody to perform well, they have to be trained. Maybe not an issue if you have an office full of 50-year-olds with PhDs and 30 years' experience of the specific task that you need them to do. Wouldn't *that* be nice? Unfortunately, in the real world, it isn't quite like that. The natural makeup of any company or team means that you may have a few of these sorts of guys, but you're also going to have a bunch of spotty graduates fresh out of university, a couple of apprentices who left school only last week, and John, who's just transferred from accounts and is a whiz with spreadsheets but knows diddlysquat about rocket science, which, unfortunately, is where you're short of people.

There are two things that are important for a manager when it comes to training. First and most obvious is that people need to be given the opportunity to go and be trained appropriately. This may be a couple of hours of being shown how to use a new piece of software or a couple of years on a postgraduate course at a local university, whatever is necessary. The budget and the time need to be made available to allow people to do so, preferably as part of a managed and coordinated, long-term career-development plan for that person.

That's the easy bit. The difficult bit is when they come back from the training, or when they have just joined your department fresh from university, for example, and they actually have to do some work. The number of times I have heard the following conversation, or a variation on it, worries me horribly. I find it so frustrating every time. Names have been changed to protect the guilty:

PERFORMANCE

SENIOR MANAGER:	How's the project going?
MANAGER:	I'm afraid we're behind schedule.
SENIOR MANAGER:	What's the problem?
MANAGER:	I just don't have enough people.
SENIOR MANAGER:	How many do you need?
MANAGER:	Another two would be a great help.
SENIOR MANAGER:	OK, I've got Fred Smith and Arthur Nigel Other coming free next week. You can have them.
MANAGER:	Ah, but I'm talking about good people.
SENIOR MANAGER:	They *are* good: they're keen and enthusiastic, with exemplary records.
MANAGER:	But they don't have any experience in Gyro Krypton Generator fusing.
SENIOR MANAGER:	But we don't have anybody available with those specific skills. Fred and Arthur can learn. They've worked with Krypton hoverjets in the past.
MANAGER:	But by the time I've brought them up to speed I could have done the job myself. There's no point in my having them.
SENIOR MANAGER:	Are you sure?
MANAGER:	Yes, I'd rather just keep on gallantly fighting a losing battle [and continue to blame you for my problems].

It's that line 'by the time I've brought them up to speed I could have done the job myself' that's the killer. Yes, in these situations you do need to spend time with people and it will be slow to start with, but it's an investment for the future that can pay back handsomely. My bet is that, in nine out of ten situations, the person speaking this line couldn't actually do the work more quickly themselves – they are usually so snowed under by the day-to-day firefighting that they would never be able to find the time. But, by not finding the short amount of time required to bring the person up to speed, they miss out on the long-term benefits of having the extra help. Coming at it from the point of view of Fred or Arthur, it's the age-old dilemma: you can't get a job without experience and you can't get experience without a job.

If we took this approach with young children we would have a nation full of juvenile delinquents. The best way for children (indeed anybody) to learn is by doing things. They need to be allowed to 'experience' on a daily basis. As a parent, therefore, you often have to put the immediate task objective to one side for a while as you focus on the developmental process instead.

One day, when Sam was still in his early days of walking, I needed to go round to the local shop to get a newspaper (Melanie would challenge the word need here, but I'm sure you know where I'm coming from). It isn't far from our house to the shop: five minutes there and five minutes back at most. Anyway, I set off holding Sam's hand while he waddled beside me down the garden path and up the

> FIND THE TIME
> TO BRING A NEW TEAM
> MEMBER UP TO SPEED,
> AND YOU'LL REAP
> THE LONG-TERM
> BENEFITS OF HAVING
> EXTRA HELP.

street. Now, ordinarily, I would have picked Sam up after a couple of minutes and carried him to the shop, maybe not achieving the five-minutes-there-and-back time, but getting pretty close. Sam, however, was really enjoying himself walking and when I went to pick him up he was having none of it, throwing his weight, in the way kids do, back at the ground with a determination that will serve him well in later life but is really inconvenient when you've got a *Sunday Times* to read.

After a couple of goes, I gave in and decided to go with the flow. What the heck – the sun was shining, the birds were tweeting and, *Sunday Times* aside, when I thought about it there was no particular rush. So off we waddled (though I would like to think that Sam was doing most of the waddling). Of course, not only was the waddling slow, but His Nibs also had to stop on a regular basis to inspect various sites of special toddler interest on the way – the bugs crawling across the pavement, a lamppost, a storm-drain grid, a weed growing out of a wall and the fastening mechanism on somebody's front gate. After half an hour we finally arrived at the shop, which, thank goodness, had not sold out of the *Sunday Times*. We then set off for home, which I estimated would be another half an hour, but unfortunately forgot that the return journey was uphill! By the time we got back to the front door, the round trip had taken a good hour and a half – a little longer than I had originally planned.

Now, as a highly competent parent or manager, you can easily take the view that the task must always be the primary focus, to the detriment of everything else. Or you can take the view that there are times when putting the task to one side in the short term will be beneficial in the long term. Thankfully, given that his walking has now progressed somewhat, these days I can walk to the same shop with Sam in something more like the standard five minutes. If people are genuinely going to be your most important asset, it's up to you to ensure that they are not treated as the cogs of some huge machine, but that the planning is carried out, the time taken and the investment made to ensure that they are developed for the long-term good of themselves and the company. If a manager expects good performance from his team, then he must also accept that he has responsibilities too.

Emotional Maturity

'I've had it with you and your emotional constipation.'

Tantor the Elephant, *Tarzan* (1999)

THE term *emotional intelligence* is becoming more common these days as it is recognised that there is more to intelligence than just being able to do hard sums. The need to be able to recognise, understand and act upon people's emotions, all things encompassed by emotional intelligence, is now seen as an important part of a manager's capability. Well, I'm going to add my own term to this concept: *emotional maturity*.

The first part of emotional maturity is the ability to be able to admit when you are wrong. In *The Sixty Minute Father*, Rob Parsons comments:

> *Children need to know that their father sometimes gets it wrong. I once heard a father boast, 'I have never, nor would I ever, apologise to my son.' You can fear a man like that – but it's hard to respect him, and even harder to have a deep relationship with him.*

Yes, admitting that you have made a mistake can be incredibly difficult, and many managers fear that if they do they will lose the respect of their team. However, I firmly believe that it has the opposite effect and increases their respect. What's far worse is somebody making a mistake and trying to cover it up, or vehemently defending a position that is indefensible just because they don't want to backtrack. Instead, the emotionally mature thing to do is to own up, and, just as importantly, show that you have learned from it.

I was once doing some work on the shop floor that occasionally involved working on the computer that was used for managing maintenance work. It was a complicated system in the days before software was foolproofed (that's my excuse anyway!) and I managed to hit the wrong key, which sent the system into meltdown. It was very tempting to switch the thing off and walk away but I decided to get the help of one of the machine operators to try to sort it out. After a lot of messing about, we finally got everything back up and working again. I apologised to him for taking up so much of his time and causing so much disruption. I expected him to shrug his shoulders and pass some patronising comment about my ineptitude, but instead he actually thanked me for being honest and having the guts to flag up what had happened. 'Most people would have just switched the thing off and walked away,' he said. Then, and since, I have never regretted owning up to my mistakes.

> OWN UP TO YOUR MISTAKES, AND FORGIVE OTHERS THEIRS.

The second aspect of emotional maturity is forgiveness, a concept too often ignored in the cut-and-thrust business of management. You'd be surprised (actually, maybe not when you think about it) at just how many people at work bear grudges towards other people. Most of the time these grudges are pretty minor, but there are plenty of times when they start to become a serious issue and get in the way of performance. I've seen some real 'grudge matches' develop between people who are very clever, experienced and capable, but, because they are unable to forgive each other for whatever it is that has caused their altercation, the working relationship spirals downwards and the results that are required from their cooperation don't materialise. When I was working as a consultant, there were once two guys on my team who just couldn't get over their differences, no matter how often we sat down to try to sort things out as 'mature adults'. It drove me crazy.

One of the amazing things about having young children is how easy it is to forgive them. No matter how naughty they've been and how cross they've made you, at the end of the day, when all's said and done, they're your kids and you love them to bits, and you can't help but forgive them for being the 'interesting little personalities' that they are. (We'll see if this still applies when they get older and less cute and cuddly.) It may not be exactly the same, but a bit of this natural forgiveness would go a long way in the workplace.

You Get What You Expect

'If you think you can, you can. And if you think you can't, you're right.'

Henry Ford

BOTH children and adults lower or raise their behaviour or performance based on what they realise is expected of them. Apparently this is known as the *Pygmalion effect*.

In an experiment that was conducted to demonstrate this, three teachers were told that they were the best in the local education authority and would therefore be given three classes of very clever and able children to teach for a year. The kids were also told that they were very clever. At the end of the year all the pupils sat exams and got really good grades. Only then were they all told (in a very pleasant way, I'm sure) that the teachers were pretty average and so were the kids.

The moral: become known as the manager who doesn't expect too much and that's what you'll get; become known as the manager who has high standards and that's what people will deliver.

TEAMS

'Great men are rarely isolated mountain-peaks: they are the summit of ranges.'

Thomas Wentworth Higginson, American soldier

I never really thought about it much at the time, but after the arrival in this world of Jack, and his safe passage through his first year, I automatically wanted another child. Fortunately, this desire was granted and Sam and Will followed. It was an almost instinctive feeling that Jack should have at least one sibling. Perhaps it is instinctive. I certainly don't think I was unusual in my feelings – there are plenty of people who I know feel the same. You have only to go to the local park to prove that. Looking at it now, and being a bit dispassionate and rational about the whole thing (I do work in industry, after all), I wonder whether it felt instinctive because we know that teamwork and getting on with other people is such an intrinsic part of life and fundamental to human progress and survival.

Perhaps putting our children into a team environment as early and as much as possible is actually instinctive for the good of the human race. Perhaps the whole process of learning how to interact with other people – understand them, collaborate with them and often compete with them – is all begun in the those early days with our siblings. One for the child psychologists to think about.

What I *am* certain about is that teams and teamwork are fundamental to any company, and managing them is pretty much what management is all about, be it a small team with only a handful of people or an enormous team of thousands.

One of the days of my career that I will never forget is when the Airbus A380 took off for its maiden flight from Toulouse. Large TV screens were erected at our office in Bristol so that everybody who had been involved in the project could watch together. Our office is a three-floor building with a large atrium in the middle. People were crowded round the balcony to the atrium on each of the three floors, and up the spiral staircase in the middle, to watch the event. The tension as the plane stood at the end of the airfield and then as it started to roll down the runway was electric. When the double-decker aircraft then slowly eased itself off the ground and into the air, the cheer that went up was comparable in size to the aeroplane itself. It was absolutely fantastic – a real adrenalin rush and really quite emotional.

There was a true sense that everybody had worked tirelessly together on the project over several years and it had all culminated in these few short seconds of joint celebration. My own part in the project was very small, but I really felt proud to be part of such a huge effort by thousands of people working across the world. It was the ultimate example of what a team of people can do when they pool their collective talent, and the result is greater than the sum of the parts.

And this is what teamwork is all about: working together to produce a something that one person could not produce on his own.

A different kind of insight came to me one day when I sat down with Jack, Sam and Will to do a jigsaw puzzle. It was quite a difficult one (lots of tricky blue sky above Thomas the Tank Engine's head) and Sam was a bit reluctant to get stuck in. When I explained that we were going to work together to help finish it, Sam yelled out excitedly, 'Yeah, we can all work as a team.' Quite impressed with his understanding of teams at such an early age, I asked if he had learned about them at school. 'No,' he said, looking at me, as he does, as if I had just crawled out from underneath a rock, 'they work in a team in *Bob the Builder*!'

Now if a four-year-old can pick up the importance of teams from a three-inch-high Plasticine builder with no fingers, then they must be important!

We Are Family

MR INCREDIBLE: I can't. I'm not strong enough.
MRS INCREDIBLE (Elastigirl):   If we work together, you won't
                                                   have to be.

The Incredibles (2004)

IT'S interesting how many successful managers talk about the importance of cultivating a sense of family among their team members. In *Leadership and the Quest for Integrity*, Joseph L. Badaracco and Richard R. Ellsworth asked a number of chief executives what the characteristics of an ideal company were:

> *The importance of shared purpose was reflected in the frequency with which these executives referred to their companies with metaphors that involved community, family, or athletic teams. Walter Writson* [chairman of Citibank] *observed, 'One reason for our success is that we have created a spirit of family.' He stressed the importance of getting people to live in each other's pockets by practising living together in all kinds of circumstances … At Johnson & Johnson, divisions were referred to as a 'family of companies'. A sense of community not only increases cohesiveness and the likelihood people will share a vision, but also fosters an environment that accepts the challenge of high standards in pursuit of that vision.*

There is definitely a general consensus among management gurus that, if you can engender some sort of family atmosphere among your team, they will work together more effectively. 'Not if it's anything like my family!' I hear you cry. And there would be many a day when I would wholeheartedly agree with you. But, if you can cut past the tantrums, the arguments about staying out late and the refusal to eat Brussels sprouts, then there are things that make this philosophy sound sensible: the shared values, the commitment to each other, the knowledge of each other's strengths and weaknesses and an invisible bond, to name a few.

There are all sorts of team-building activities that people use to try to facilitate this process – ten-pin bowling, Outward Bound courses, meals out, go-karting and many more. Unfortunately, however, in many respects, the best way for this sense of family to develop is for everybody to go through some sort of real crisis together, rather than perform some artificial exercise. This really is the best way to pull people together.

A couple of years ago I was managing a team that had to deliver a whole bunch of documentation to Airbus headquarters in Toulouse by a certain date, and, as with all good projects, we were running right up against the deadline. The day before the deadline fell, things were getting really tight and the whole team were running round frantically, desperately trying to

> TEAMS WITH A SENSE OF FAMILY KNOW INSTINCTIVELY WHAT THEIR COLLEAGUES THINK, WANT AND DO.

pull together, literally thousands of sheets of paper that had to be written up, printed and collated. As the day wore on it was clear that it was going to be a late finish to get everything done before the next day. The evening then wore on, the night wore on and the early morning wore on.

The camaraderie that developed, though, as the situation became more and more unusual, was quite noticeable. In one night, the team bonded far more than it had ever done over the previous 12 months. People went out to get fish and chips at two in the morning to keep everybody else going; the jokes were flying left, right and centre; and there was 100 per cent focus on getting the job done. By four o'clock everything was completed. I went home, had a shower, and immediately left again to catch the 6.45 am plane to Toulouse to hand-deliver the stuff. It wasn't pretty, but the job had been done and my team were much stronger for it.

It is a bit difficult, though, waiting for these sorts of moments to come round. This is one of the reasons why teams are often sent on Ourward Bound courses – to put people in artificial situations that accelerate this bonding process. In fact, this bonding process is so important that a very clever man called Bruce Tuckman has actually broken it down into defined stages: *forming, storming, norming* and *performing*.

- **Forming:** This is when people don't know each other very well and are gaining ideas from each other on what problems need solving and how.
- **Storming:** They then go through a phase of storming – a necessary period of conflict when differences come to the surface and personalities can clash.
- **Norming:** The team then find some common ground and agree on a way forward.
- **Performing:** Norming has enabled them to move into the final stage of performing, when the team are working efficiently and the problem is solved.

By going through this bonding process, individuals cease to become islands of output and start to work as an effective team, multiplying their output many times. Teams that have worked together long enough and have been through this process several times can then start to develop a sense of family, whereby team members know instinctively what their colleagues think, want and do. If you can develop this sense of family in your own team, it will pay you back handsomely.

One For All and All For One

'The team with the best athletes doesn't usually win. It's the team with the athletes who play best together.'

Lisa Fernandez, softball player

ONE of the great changes that you go through when you become a parent is a drastic overhaul of the selfish side of your character. Almost overnight (or over two nights if your partner has a particularly unlucky labour) you change from somebody who has a pretty high focus on making sure that Number One is happy to somebody whose total focus is on making sure that the newly arrived bundle of loveliness is safe and happy. All it can do is sleep, cry, vomit and fill its nappy with substances of various colours and consistencies, and it has your total dedication. Just imagine being as devoted to your partner if that were all the activity they could muster!

And it isn't just when they are cute and gurgly (I'm back to the child now, not your partner) – throughout childhood and beyond, a parent is constantly worrying for, and wanting the best for, their children. Your whole life becomes focused on doing what is best for them, be it in terms of their education, where you go on holiday or what you do for Christmas. When the parents get older, of course, and the children are grown up, then the roles are often reversed and it becomes the children wanting the best for their parents (got that, kids?). There are people who say that this is the whole point and that everybody is acting selfishly really. But, whatever the long-term, deep, psychological drivers, members of a family generally look after each other.

Managing a team requires just the same approach. The World War II American supreme commander General Douglas MacArthur once said that the greatest asset a leader can have is the care of the people under his command and the ability to show that care. If your team members feel that you are using them for purely selfish reasons, then they are not going to perform in the way you want them to.

Trampling all over people in order to get that promotion you've always wanted will not work in the long run. You will soon be found out. Everybody in your team needs to feel that they are 'in it together' and that they are working for the overall good of the team. Not for you, or for themselves, but for the team as a whole.

One of the ways of doing this is by making sure that people are involved as much as possible and at the very least have an input into the decision making, even if they are not able to make the decisions themselves. If team members are just told what to do the whole time, then they are soon going to feel as if they were working purely for your benefit and not everybody's. If, however, people can see that it is the team's performance and result that are important, and that the glory will be shared, they will be far more willing to slog their guts out.

> EVERYBODY IN YOUR TEAM NEEDS TO FEEL THAT THEY ARE 'IN IT TOGETHER'.

If you can engender this within your team, it can be very powerful. Rather than wait to be told what to do by you, people will feel empowered to take action and work towards the best result, since they know that it will be for the good of everybody. One of the things that really grate on me is when people disagree with something that's happening within their company and say that '*they* have gone and done this' or '*they* have decided that', as if the company were controlled and run by some anonymous group of aliens who speak a foreign language. If a proper sense of team existed in the company, and those individuals felt as if they were part of that team, instead of grumbling they would go and air their differences and have a debate about the issue with the appropriate person. A company is just a large team, and is made up of all its employees. As within any team, everybody should feel they are part of it and are responsible for its wellbeing.

There is an *I* in 'Team'!

'Cherish forever what makes you unique, cuz you're really a yawn if it goes.'

Bette Midler

ONE of the secrets of building a strong team is to have the right balance of people in the group, though it is rare to have the opportunity to pick a team from scratch. Most managers inherit an existing team or are 'given' a group of people to work with rather than having the luxury of creating a team from a blank sheet of paper. No matter how you come by your team, though, it's important to understand the individuals who make it up. Just because people are working in a team and for the common good, it doesn't mean that they lose their individuality and that you shouldn't be aware of people's individual characteristics and personalities.

It's just the same for a parent. No two kids in a family are the same, no matter how much you try to bring them up the same. It's fascinating to observe the differences among our three. Meal times with visiting grandparents are usually spent analysing their different behaviours and characters. As their personalities develop, you learn what makes each one tick and what works for one but not for another, their different likes and dislikes, strengths and weaknesses. Even though you're a family, each individual family member plays their own role.

There are a number of techniques that have been devised within businesses to try to make this process scientific in the workplace. There can't be many people these days who haven't gone on a training course where they have had to fill in some sort of personality questionnaire in order to determine how they operate as an individual within a team. Probably one of the best known of these is the Belbin Team Role Questionnaire. Participants are asked to complete a simple questionnaire and the results are then analysed to determine which of nine different team roles the person fits into. Each role is given a snappy title – Implementer, Coordinator, Shaper, Plant, Resource Investigator, Monitor-Evaluator, Team Worker, Completer and Specialist. The idea is that, for a team to be effective, it needs a spread of people with skills across the range of these types. For example, if a team has loads of Coordinators and no Implementers, nothing gets done and the Coordinators have nothing to coordinate. Also, depending on which type they fall under, different people may have a clash of personalities that can lead to friction in the team.

> JUST BECAUSE PEOPLE ARE WORKING IN A TEAM AND FOR THE COMMON GOOD, IT DOESN'T MEAN THAT THEY LOSE THEIR INDIVIDUALITY.

For some people, this type of theory starts to become quite controversial and various objections along the lines of 'you can't put people in boxes' are aired. I was on a course once where this technique was used and a particularly religious woman stormed out of the room claiming it was unethical and evil! While I personally wouldn't go quite as far as this, I do agree that it is a huge simplification of the diversity of humankind and needs to be used as a interesting guide rather than a definitive scientific tool.

What it does highlight, though, is that people are different, and understanding those differences is important when you are building and managing a team. I think it needs more intuition and emotional intelligence to understand properly what makes people tick, rather than deciding which of nine types they fit into. However, you do need to ensure that you understand and are aware of the characteristics and habits of the different individuals in your team.

Once you have done this, it's a case of making sure you give people in the team clearly defined roles that are appropriate to them. I remember when I was a child that there was a rota stuck up in the kitchen with a clear allocation of jobs among my brother, my sister and me, to be carried out each evening after dinner. We then reluctantly carried out the allocated task before being allowed to run off to watch the TV or beat each other up, depending on our mood.

It sounds a bit obvious, but in any team people need to know what they are doing, and also why. All team members need to have a clearly defined role: (a) to avoid duplication of effort and (b) so they are clear and motivated about what they are doing. Without this, the work effort of the team is going to be pretty poor. A clear and communicated organisation-breakdown structure is therefore important to show the makeup of the team and who is doing what.

Finally, you need to remember that people are not static and their behaviours will change over time as their circumstances change. In the way that you wouldn't treat your 15-year-old son in the same way that you did when he was five, you wouldn't want to manage an experienced team member in the same way that you needed to when they first joined the team and were finding their feet. It's a continuous process of observing, learning, understanding and adapting how you work with the same people over time. As with your children, it never stops.

CHANGE

'There is nothing more difficult to take in hand, more perilous to conduct, or more uncertain in its success, than to take the lead in the introduction of a new order of things, because the innovator has for enemies all those who have done well under the old conditions, and lukewarm defenders in those who may do well under the new.'

Niccolò Machiavelli, Italian political philosopher,
The Prince (Il Principe)

DEPENDING on your particular management role, the amount of change that you will be required to manage will vary. Some roles are about nothing other than implementing change in order to improve the way things are done. Other roles are more about managing the day-to-day, and will be less concerned with change. Even in these sorts of role, though, there will be times when change is introduced and needs to be managed.

Change is happening all of the time to all of us. Sometimes it's slow, incremental change and sometimes it's big, life-transforming stuff. It might be introducing a new checking procedure on a production line or it might be introducing a new strategy across a multinational corporation. No matter what the size of the change, though, two things are common: change is difficult and people don't like it.

I was once managing a project in which I was looking to change a process that involved a number of people. An IT system used to order parts was being expanded and was going to be implemented in an area that had previously used a paper system. As a result, the ordering process needed changing to be aligned with the capabilities of the software.

I was being met with all sorts of resistance. It was all too difficult and people didn't have the time. Apparently, there were all sorts of disadvantages in going to the new process and reasons why the current process should be retained. During one of the meetings to discuss the project with the people involved, it transpired that one of the changes I was looking to introduce was actually going back to a method that had been used in the past. I had been completely unaware of this. One chap in the meeting, who was providing his fair share of resistance to what was going on, told me how, when the change had originally been made, he didn't think the new method was a good idea, but now he liked it and didn't think that changing back to the original method was a good idea either. I smiled to myself. It was obvious to me that the intricacies of which method was the better one were not the issue here: it was simply the process of going through the change itself.

Comfort Blankets

RAFIKI: Ah, change is good.
SIMBA: Yeah, but it's not easy.

The Lion King (1994)

THE first lesson for managing change is to expect resistance. You will meet it. But why do people resist change and make it so difficult?

I have a theory.

Babies like routine. As I said earlier, there are varying trains of thought over exactly how much routine, but even the most 'relaxed' of babies is encouraged to be asleep at some point during the night and to feed on some sort of regular basis. There are plenty of childcare experts who advocate quite a structured routine, though. In her book *The Contented Little Baby Book*, Gina Ford lays out a routine for newborn babies that maps out each 24 hours down to the last minute. I kid you not. Dr Christopher Green, in *Toddler Taming*, is more pragmatic:

> *Little children tend to be much more secure and happy when they live in an organised, structured environment. As well as knowing when they are going to be fed, when it is bedtime, and when it is time to go to pre-school, they also need to know the behavioural limits that their parents will tolerate. Most children thrive on routine and will immediately be thrown out of kilter by late nights, late meals, unexpected visitors or mum or dad going away on business.*

We certainly found that, when our three were babies, a pretty consistent routine worked very well. As a result, on the sleeping front at least, they've all generally been pretty good. We definitely found it of benefit ourselves as well. Certainly with your first child, it at least gives some sort of order to a life that has just been completely turned upside down. But for the baby, too, it provides stability and order. They know that they're going to be fed and that they're going to get a sleep when they need it.

We found, though, that when the routine got broken – for whatever reason – we were slowly left with a more and more unhappy baby. When we went away, you would see a marked change in their behaviour as they struggled with changes to their routine and the change in their environment. When Will was a small baby, without fail, when we went away, he would gradually eat less and less at mealtimes, until, after three or four days, getting anything down his gullet was almost impossible. Fortunately, we were never away long enough for this to become a problem.

As children get older, even though the routine of sleeping and feeding becomes less of an issue, they follow a routine nonetheless. Get up, have breakfast, go to school, do sums, have lunch, do spelling, go home, have tea, have bath, have story, go to bed.

Perhaps, therefore, having had routine established as an integral part of our lives, almost from Day One, we find it more difficult to cope with change. By the time we're adults, it has pretty much been conditioned out of us. It's no wonder that any upset to our status quo is treated with scepticism and resisted at all costs. We are taught to dislike change.

In fact, we dislike it so much that we often try to pretend it isn't happening. I assume that people are so afraid of change and of the unknown that this is the only way they can deal with it.

A university housemate of mine, unintentionally, helped illustrate this point perfectly. I was going to a black-tie party with a few friends and we were all in a department store shopping for, well, black ties. As we were making our way to the men's evening-wear section, we passed through the ladies' swimwear section. As you do.

Now, my housemate, a very intelligent and subsequently successful individual, had a penchant for doing odd and plain silly things in public. Nothing particularly crazy, just silly. On this occasion, for reasons best known only to himself, he decided that he was going to parade round the floor of the department store wearing a hat that he had spotted. The hat in question was one of those garish rubber swimming caps, festooned with multicoloured rubber flowers, that only 60-year-old women doing a sedate breaststroke in the slow lane of the public baths ever wear.

It was all mildly amusing (you didn't want to encourage him) and we had a bit of a giggle as he walked around making a fool of himself. But then we noticed that he *wasn't* making a fool of himself. Nobody else really batted an eyelid. It wasn't that they hadn't noticed him, because he did look pretty stupid, what with the swimming cap and his five o'clock shadow. People just didn't seem to be able to compute that here

> ## WE ARE TAUGHT TO DISLIKE CHANGE.

was something different and odd. My housemate walked around for quite some time and people just didn't react.

I am quite a fan of Channel 4's *Trigger Happy TV*, and anybody who has ever watched Dom Joly doing stupid things to unsuspecting members of the public will have seen very similar, but much funnier, situations. When people are going about their daily lives and are in their 'routine', they just don't react to something out of the ordinary in the way that you would have thought they would. They just carry on being normal, presumably because that is what we are all programmed to do. I guess that, for carrying out everyday tasks, this programming is really useful, because it allows us to do lots of things without having to think too much. Driving a car is a very good example. When it comes to change, though, this programming works against us and it takes a while for us to accept that we can't continue to rely on the comfort of our routines.

It's About People, Silly

> 'But people do change ... you'd be surprised how much I changed for your mother.'

The King, *Shrek 2* (2004)

DURING my career, especially when I was in consulting, I have worked on a number of change programmes, in particular ones involving the implementation of a new 'revolutionising' computer system. Anybody who is involved in these sorts of improvement initiatives will tell you the same thing. Their success is not dependent upon how clever the new strategy is, or how much money is spent on the programme, or how many bells and whistles the new IT software comes with, or whether the project has a wacky name. The critical factor is always how well the people involved are managed through the change. You can have the sexiest IT system in the world, but if you ignore the people using it then you will never reap any benefits. Management consultancies have whole departments full of sensitive people who are experts in the people side of change programmes, because they recognise its importance to the success of these types of projects.

So if change is all about people and people hate change, so much that they would rather ignore it, what's a manager to do? I have a few suggestions.

1. Have a Vision

> 'It's kind of fun to do the impossible.'

Walt Disney

The first thing to be clear of in your own mind, or as a company, is what the change is all about. Where is it taking you and why will it be better to be there rather than where you are today? What is the vision? If there is no vision, you would have to question why you're bothering to go through the hassle of all the change in the first place, given how difficult we've decided it's going to be.

Imagine deciding to move house to the other end of the country when your teenage son has just met his first girlfriend and your teenage daughter has friends all over the locality who have sworn eternal allegiance to each other (in the ways girls do, I'm sure). If your reason for moving was, 'Well your mum and I fancied something a bit different and they've got a good Sainsbury's in Aberdeen ...', then you're going to have a difficult time selling it. And an even more difficult time living with the kids when you get there.

There has to be a clear and justifiable reason for going through the change, and people have to be able to recognise when they've come out the other end.

2. Talk to People

> 'You don't have to be the Dalai Lama to tell people that life's about change.'
>
> John Cleese

It's a cliché to say that good communication is important. But when you're taking people through change it's especially important. Having formed a vision, people need to know what it is. They also need to know how you're going to take them there, how long it's going to take, what will be different, what will be their role, whether they'll be all right, what the risks are, who else is involved, what the alternative is, whether they will they lose out financially. The list goes on and on.

Thinking through what you need to tell people and telling them upfront in an open and honest way is crucial. Even better, where possible, involve them in deciding what is the best way to change. People literally become scared when they are going through change. If they feel they are being kept in the dark or, even worse, deceived, you will lose them.

I mentioned going away with our children when they were babies and the fact that it noticeably unsettled them. Sam, even when he was well into the toddler years, would withdraw into himself when we were staying at somebody else's house (these days he just wrecks the joint). Some advice we were given was that, as soon as they were old enough to be able to understand, it was important to explain to the children what you were about to do. Just chucking them in the car and driving up the M6 for three hours was bound to confuse them. If you explained beforehand that they were going to see Nanna and Grandpa, that they'd be in the car for a long journey and would be sleeping in a different bed tonight, but that it was all going to be very exciting, they would be far more prepared for the upheaval.

> **THERE HAS TO BE A CLEAR AND JUSTIFIABLE REASON FOR MAKING A CHANGE AND PEOPLE HAVE TO BE ABLE TO RECOGNISE WHEN THEY'VE COME OUT THE OTHER END.**

Recognising that this was an upheaval for them was also important. Going away for a couple of nights for us was no big deal, but for somebody who's two and a half feet tall and likes his cuddly frog in bed at night, it is. In *Raising Happy Children*, Jan Parker and Jan Stimpson write about this need to explain change to children. Their words, though, could just as well be written about adults.

> *There is a fear in the unknown. Much avoidable stress and anxiety is caused by children not understanding what is going on in their lives. Why are they feeling as they do? Why are they in this situation? Where will it lead? Confusion can bewilder, frighten and crush a child's ability to find her own way through a situation or problem.*
>
> *Talking with your child about any significant and imminent change in her life will help her negotiate it more successfully. Try not to inflate it beyond its reasonable significance or tell her what she will or should feel about it, but rather give her the information she needs to understand what is happening.*

What might seem like insignificant change to you may actually be very significant for your team, and they will need to discuss it and understand it with you.

3. Take Your Time

'I was taught that the way of progress is neither swift nor easy.'

Marie Curie, scientist

There will be times when carrying out change has to be done in a quick and 'big bang' type of approach, I don't deny that. However, for change to be successful, and for it to be lasting, it is far better if it can be carried out incrementally and steadily. Change that is rushed and 'dumped' on people is usually the change that fails.

For me, evolution is better than revolution.

One of the things that always amazes me about children is that, day on day, there is no perceptible change in their development. Look at a child one day, put him to bed and get him up the following day, and he looks pretty much identical and is doing pretty much exactly the same things as he was the day before. Yet, over time, he changes from a crying bundle of gurgliness, with no teeth, no hair, no bowel or bladder control, no speech and weighing a few pounds into a six-foot brain surgeon who can play the piano, read Shakespeare and do the Rubik's cube.

I think there's a lesson in that.

MANAGING
YOURSELF

'Love a lot, trust a few, but always paddle your own canoe.'

Painted on the back of a lorry, M5 southbound,
Gloucestershire

INTERESTINGLY, managers need to understand and 'manage' themselves just as much as they manage other people. By having a grasp of their own strengths, weakness and development needs, managers are in a stronger position to manage their team. In *The Way to Win*, Will Carling and Robert Heller say,

> *Self-mastery is the key to mastery in any sport or management activity. Paradoxically, time spent on developing individual skills and attitudes pays off in terms of more effective work with others. One vital skill is thinking about yourself.*

You should therefore not take the fact that this is the last part of the book as an indication of its importance. I've left it till last so that it is the one that you remember most. I hope it will still stick in your mind when you have finished the book (and put it under you desk leg to sort out that slight wobble that's been irritating you for years). The above advice, to take time out to think about yourself, is good advice. Understanding yourself, what makes you tick, what you're good at, what you're not good at and what you want out of life is an important aspect of being a manager. Hopefully this section will help that process in some small way. The rest is up to you.

It's All in the Mind

'It is our choices, Harry, that show what we truly are, far more than our abilities.'

Professor Albus Dumbledore,
Harry Potter and the Chamber of Secrets

I will never forget the first time my parents visited us after Jack was born. I opened the door to them with Jack in my arms and was treated to an eternity of ooing and cooing by the new grandparents. OK, a couple of minutes. Later on, my father and I had to go and pick up a new tumble dryer from a nearby shop – an essential item for parents who want to use washable nappies! It was when we got back to the house and started manhandling the thing out of the back of the car that for some reason I was completely overcome by a huge sense of responsibility. Here I was, no longer just a son, the youngest generation of the family, but now elevated to position of father. And my own dad was now a grandpa. Bizarre.

Rather than coming home to my wife and some decorating, which had been the general state of affairs for the previous two or three years, I was coming home to a seven-day-old baby who was totally and utterly dependent on us, but who, unfortunately, had not come with any instructions (unlike the tumble dryer, which proved to be far more straightforward to operate). It sounds a bit soppy now, but I really was totally overawed by the situation and my new position in the extended family.

It can be very similar when you first become a manager, or when you start in a new management role. The enormity of what you're taking on, and just how much you don't know, can be overwhelming. This is what I call the pea-soup phase of a job. There are all sorts of issues that need sorting out but it's difficult to get a grasp on anything, especially when you just don't understand most of it. Everyone's looking to you for answers and you're thinking to yourself, what the hell do I do?

Nothing makes sense, but you're supposed to be the one in charge. Being successful in this situation and coming out the other side, on top, is not just about your managerial capability and talent, though: it's also about your confidence.

When you start a managerial role, and as you face the ongoing challenges that you encounter as a manager, your self-confidence will be tested to its limit. It's crucial for all managers to develop and maintain a strong self-belief. Easy to say, and for some people easy to do. For others, it can be much harder. But managers who do have strong self-belief are able to ride out the sorts of circumstances I've described above and come out the other side in control and in charge.

In *The Way to Win*, Will Carling and Robert Heller talk about the total self-belief that Daley Thompson, the Olympic decathlete, had in himself. Thompson tackled everything from the point of view that he was good until proven otherwise, unlike most people, who think that they're not and hope for a surprise. He wasn't arrogant, just confident. This total self-belief, coupled with a gruelling training programme that included two training sessions on Christmas Day, is what Thompson believed gave him the mental edge over his competitors, some of whom were technically better than he was. Thompson's self-confidence was so high he almost felt he deserved to beat his competitors. And he did.

But it's easy to be self-confident if you *are* self-confident. What if you're not?

First, you need to decide that you're going to be confident. It's as easy as that. It's almost as if you need to trip a mental switch in your head that might take only a millisecond to do, but can change your whole mindset for ever. Most people who struggle with something have already decided that they can't do it before they even try. People who struggle at maths decided in the first year of school that they couldn't add up. People who are broke have always thought that they are hopeless with money. And so it goes on. If you're going into something with a picture in your mind that says you are going to fail, then you will.

Second, *act* confident. If you adopt the physical characteristics of somebody who is confident, then you will actually become more confident yourself. Speak clearly, use a strong tone of voice, talk directly to people, maintain direct eye contact, stand upright. I was once asked to carry out an exercise on a training course where I had to describe to another person my previous day's activities while adopting a depressed, cold and meek style. By the end of the exercise I felt as though I had had a pretty awful day, even though it was actually pretty normal. The exercise was then

> IT'S CRUCIAL FOR ALL MANAGERS TO DEVELOP AND MAINTAIN A STRONG SELF-BELIEF.

repeated, but this time adopting a positive, happy and vivacious style. And – lo and behold! – the previous day suddenly felt as if it had been a lot better.

This technique has been shown to work by researchers who have given college students scripts to act out in a confident manner. The researchers found that, over time, the students were able to learn how to be more confident, and that, when they subsequently found themselves managing a team, the team's performance was better than when it was managed by an unconfident leader. If, therefore, you walk around with big strides, sit up straight, actively talk firmly, play loud music in the car, think positive, then you will find that you do actually become more confident.

If you're unable to get over low self-confidence, though, you not only shy away from difficult decisions or actions, but also withdraw from your team. They sense your lack of self-belief and take on the same behaviour. It's exactly the same with young children. Earlier, I talked about how children pick up on even the smallest of signs that their parents transmit. If you're nervous about taking them swimming for the first time, then they will pick up on your lack of confidence and become nervous too. People are very aware, if only subconsciously, of the aura, or lack of it, that we give off to the outside world.

Think of Daley Thompson, and make sure your aura is a positive one.

Delegate

'No man will make a great leader who wants to do it all himself, or to get all the credit for doing it.'

Andrew Carnegie, Scottish-born American
businessman and philanthropist

ONE of the biggest mistakes that managers make, especially new ones, is to fail to delegate. Delegation is a key skill for a very good reason. If you don't delegate, you become a bottleneck, nothing gets done and you fail. This can be a hard concept to grasp if you've just been promoted to manager and you're used to being one of the guys with a task to do, who gets his nose to the grindstone to get it done. It can be very tempting once you're a manager to gather tasks and do the same, especially if you know you've got the skills to do them and know how to get to the answer yourself.

Also, if you suffer from the 'it's quicker to do it myself' syndrome that I discussed earlier, there's a good chance that your to-do list will start to accumulate tasks more quickly than you are able to knock them off. It is even easier to fall into this trap if you are conscious that you don't want people to feel that you are work-shy, and you want your team to see that you are mucking in and doing your fair share. It just doesn't work like that, though. Managers are there to manage, not to do. It is no use complaining how overworked you are and how many meetings you have to attend or reports to write before the end of the week. You need to learn how to share out the workload. Put aside all those fears of losing control or that other people will not be able to do as good a job as you. Delegating is important.

As well as freeing up your time and allowing you to concentrate on the overall management of your team, delegating also means that your people have an opportunity to build on their existing skills and to develop new ones. As a result, they feel more involved and team morale is improved. Conversely, if they feel that you don't trust them with the work, spirits are going to fall. Better decisions will also get made, with the right guidance, because people who are involved in the detail and have the time to explore all the avenues will be making them, or helping you to make them.

Be careful of 'dumping', though. As opposed to the managed and planned activity of delegating, dumping is unplanned and chaotic and usually involves landing somebody else in a mess in a vain attempt to get yourself out of one.

Writing in *You're in Charge Now,* Julie-Ann Amos provides some useful advice when it comes to delegating: make sure you understand the person you are delegating to and their capabilities; make sure you brief them clearly; make sure you are always available to provide advice; make sure you frequently check on progress but not so often that you interfere.

The only thing that I would add is that it is a good idea to try to delegate complete jobs, rather than bits of jobs. It is much more satisfying to work on a single, complete task than on many fragments of tasks. If you delegate a complete task to a capable team member, you are more likely to receive back a more elegant and tightly integrated solution.

It doesn't end there, though. One of the hardest things I have found with delegated tasks is making sure that you don't 'undelegate' them. This is especially the case when you have delegated a task to somebody who is unfamiliar with the work or is less capable than they should be, or would rather not be doing the task in the first place. In these situations, people come back to you with problems, issues and clarifications and it can be very tempting simply to take back the task, or at least one part of it, adding to your already lengthy list of jobs. Getting good at not 'accepting the monkey', therefore, is important. Instead, talk through the issue with your team member in order to find out what they need to do next, not what you need to do.

This is very similar to a parenting technique called *active listening*, which is used to lead children to sort out, and take ownership of, their own problems, rather than lecturing them on what Mum and Dad thinks best. In the long run, the child also benefits from having solved the problem themselves.

My own father was a master at this technique, though more in the area of helping with homework than sorting out personal problems. If I ever had a question with my homework, he would never just give me the answer. Oh, no: we would have to go through the excruciating process of starting from first principles and slowly working it all through until I finally worked out the answer myself. It got to the stage where I would start my request with, 'I know you'll want me to figure this out for myself, but please, please just give me the answer – I've got a childhood to enjoy.' He never did. It was painful at the time, but I secretly thank him for it now.

> IF YOU DON'T DELEGATE, YOU BECOME A BOTTLENECK AND NOTHING GETS DONE.

Using active listening with somebody who's carrying out a piece of work for you will also lead to a better result all round. If you just take the delegated task back as soon as your team member comes up against problems, then you suffer with the extra work (both in the short and the long term) and they have missed a learning opportunity. This isn't something that is easy and is definitely something that needs a lot of practice. Getting it right, though, is in everybody's interest.

Finally, remember that it is the task that you are delegating, not the accountability. At the end of the day, you have to stand up and be counted when the results of the work are used in anger. It is worthwhile, therefore, taking the time to get delegating right.

Do It Now

'Take time to deliberate, but when the time for action has arrived, stop thinking and go in.'

Napoleon Bonaparte

I was once working on a project where things were not going well. The delivery date for the project was still six months away but it was obvious from the state of affairs that the chances of meeting that delivery date were looking pretty slim. Suppliers were late, scopes had changed, I had lost team members to other projects, unforeseen technical problems had occurred – all the usual stuff. I sat down with my boss at the time and explained the situation and that things were not looking good. He gave me a very good piece of advice. 'Ian,' he said, 'you need to work out what you can do now, that in six months' time, if you hadn't done it, you'd look back and say, "I wish I *had* done that."'

Now this seems a bit obvious, but it's true. So often, we can be so overwhelmed by the size of an issue that we just don't know where to start. Any action seems irrelevant and futile. However, there is always something that can be done – it's just a case of deciding what it is and getting on and doing it. Worrying about something gets you nowhere. In fact, it takes you backwards, not forwards. My mum has a little note on her fridge door that says, 'Face it, fix it, forget it.' Good advice, Mum.

Jack, Sam and Will have all developed a penchant for castles. Anywhere we go these days, it is almost compulsory to visit the local castle. If you could buy shares in English Heritage, I would. It is not surprising, therefore, that, when they were bombarded by adverts for toys prior to last Christmas, the advert for Lego Knights' Kingdom caught their attention. 'Daddy, can we have a Lego Knights' Kingdom?' 'Daddy, please can we have a Lego

Knights' Kingdom?' 'Daddy, we would really like a Lego Knights' Kingdom.' 'Daddy, we *need* a Lego Knights' Kingdom.' It was too much – I gave in.

Christmas Day came and, thankfully, the wretched Lego Knights' Kingdom went down a treat. That is, until they opened the box. What the advert had omitted to say was that the recommended age for the product was somewhere in the high twenties – preferably with a PhD in civil engineering. The box was full of plastic bags containing what appeared to be thousands of small pieces of Lego and an instruction 'booklet' that had clearly required the sacrifice of several large trees. The boys looked overawed. I looked overawed. Fortunately, though, Grandpa was staying for Christmas. Hallelujah!

Needing no prompting whatsoever, Grandpa laid out the bags in order and turned to Page 1 of the 'booklet'. 'Jack, open Bag 1 and put the brick 226 on foundation C.' To both Grandpa's and the children's credit, over the next two days they painstakingly put together, piece by piece, the whole Lego Knights' Kingdom. As the final turkey sandwich was being polished off at the end of Boxing Day, flag 12a was placed on top

> WE CAN BE GET SO OVERWHELMED BY THE SIZE OF AN ISSUE THAT WE DON'T KNOW WHERE TO START. BUT THERE IS ALWAYS SOMETHING THAT CAN BE DONE.

of turret P, and the Lego Knights' Kingdom was complete. We hadn't seen Grandpa or his three grandsons for two days (nobody was complaining, mind you), but it was finished.

MANAGING YOURSELF

At work, I'm afraid you don't get Page 1 of the instruction booklet handed to you – you have to work out what it looks like for yourself. But, once you have, get stuck in. What you do today does make a difference.

Get a Mentor

'Grandma we love you, Grandma we do.'

St Winifred's School Choir

I can't wait to be a grandparent. It's clearly the ideal role when it comes to children. You rock up at your grandchildren's house once in a while, spoil them hopelessly, make a big fuss, hold their undivided attention, play a few games, enjoy good behaviour on a scale previously unheard of, get raised to the level of a minor demigod and then hand them back to return home for a well-earned rest and several cups of tea.

Sounds good to me. No telling off, changing nappies, dressing, telling off, undressing, saying 'don't do that', getting up in the middle of the night, telling off, feeding, washing, telling off, ferrying to school, wiping bottoms, wiping noses or telling off. All the good bits, none of the rubbish.

Usually, as a result, the relationship between grandparent and grandchild is a pretty special one. Certainly our three idolise theirs – Grandpa with his model trains, Granddad the human climbing frame, Nanna's games and Grandma's trifle. I certainly don't begrudge them their position, though. The fact that they are separate from all of the humdrum of daily life is really good. I know from my own grandparents that having somebody there to whom you can look for independent advice is a real benefit. The fact that they aren't the people who have the unfortunate task of trying to drag you up into some sort of passable human being that can be tolerated by society, day in, day out, is a major advantage.

My own grandfather has been a constant source of inspiration to me and a real mentor. Unwittingly, over the years, he has taught me a huge amount about hard work, relationships, careers, society

> TAPPING INTO THE WISDOM OF SOMEBODY WITH EXPERIENCE, WHO HAS BEEN THROUGH THINGS THEMSELVES, CAN BRING ALL SORTS OF FRESH IDEAS AND APPROACHES TO YOUR PROBLEMS AND DECISIONS.

and how to laugh. I will never forget the magazine article he showed me when I was a boy that argued that we have too many words in the English language and that you could get by just as easily with a more limited number and using these to make up the rest where necessary. There was a short essay written using this technique. In it, for example, 'all of a sudden' became 'oil offer sodden'. It had me in stitches. He still sends me journal articles in the post today to give me some useful pointers in my career.

I know for certain that, if he had been the one having to tell me off on a daily basis, the relationship would never have been the same and I wouldn't have looked to him in the same way. Apparently, I'm not alone. In an NSPCC survey, 78 per cent of children said their grandparents were important to them.

In *Raising Boys*, Steve Biddulph talks extensively about how important this mentoring process is for boys and how they need male mentors to give them independent advice, show an interest in them, ask them questions, be there as a teacher and a coach and help them move into the larger world. He encourages parents to identify people who can suitably fill this role for their sons. He tells a poignant story to explain why:

Nat was fifteen, and his life was not going well. He had always hated school and found writing difficult, and things were just mounting up. The school he went to was a caring school, and his parents, the counsellor and the principal knew each other and could talk comfortably. They met and decided that if Nat could find a job, they would arrange an exemption. Perhaps he was one of those boys who would be happier in the adult world than the in-between world of high school.

Luckily Nat scored a job, in a one-man pizza shop – 'Stan's Pizza' – and left school. Stan, who was about thirty-five, was doing a good trade and needed help. Nat went to work there and loved it. His voice deepened, he stood taller, his bank balance grew. His parents, though, began to worry for a new reason. Nat planned to buy a motorbike – a big bike – to get to work. Their home was up a winding, slippery road in the mountains. They watched in horror as his savings got closer to the price of the motorcycle. They suggested a car, to no avail. Time passed.

One day Nat came home and, in the way of teenage boys, muttered something sideways as he walked past the dinner table. Something about a car. They asked him to repeat it, not sure if they should. 'Oh, I'm not going to get a bike. I was talking to Stan. Stan reckons a bloke'd be an idiot to buy a motorbike living up here. He reckons I should wait an' get a car.'

'Thank God for Stan!' thought his parents.

A mentor at work is equally valuable. There's no formula for the ideal mentor, but try to find a senior member of the organisation whom you respect, who knows the organisation well and preferably is not involved directly in your own day-to-day job or career progression. It should be somebody that you see as 'successful' and of whom you can ask the question, 'So how did you do that?' It's a good idea if it's somebody that you get on well with, too. You don't necessarily have to enter into any formal relationship; you don't even have to tell them they're your mentor, as long as there's some mechanism by which the two of you meet on a reasonably frequent basis. What you do need to do is to have a relationship with this person that enables you to discuss informally your work and career with them. You need to be able to look to them for independent advice, to help you look at problems, guide you through difficult periods and make challenging decisions. The benefits are huge. Tapping into the wisdom of somebody with experience, who's been through things themselves, can bring all sorts of fresh ideas and approaches to your problems or decisions, be they about a specific issue within your day job or about a significant long-term career move. They've probably been through the same situation themselves and can give you pointers and advice, having come out the other side. They may well know other people you could go and talk to about specific situations or will have information from the upper echelons of the company that you wouldn't otherwise have had access to. The fact that they are not bogged down in the weeds of your everyday issues means they can be much more objective in their advice.

And don't think that it's just a one-way process. Good mentors see their role as a learning experience for themselves, too, as a way of getting *your* view on *their* problems and issues, a way of understanding the sorts of things somebody more junior in the company is facing and as a way of seeing the organisation from a different perspective. Mentoring is a two-way process in which both parties can learn from each other.

So don't worry if you feel that you're doing all the taking from the relationship. Good mentors will do their fair share, too!

Copy the Good Stuff

'Ooh, ooh, I wanna be like you …'

Baloo, *The Jungle Book* (1967)

AS well as getting yourself a mentor, identifying role models around your business is a useful practice, too – people to whom you can relate and who are in a similar position to yourself but at a slightly higher level. People you would like to be like in a few years' time. And, once you find them, copy them. You can develop your skills enormously by observing other people, seeing what makes them successful and adopting those behaviours yourself. And it's all for free.

Top footballers watch hours of football on TV so that they can understand what good players do that distinguish them from the not-so-good players. They then adopt these moves on the pitch themselves. Rather than saying, 'I know everything', they recognise that there is still plenty they can learn from other players in order to improve the weaknesses in their own game.

> YOU CAN DEVELOP YOUR SKILLS ENORMOUSLY BY OBSERVING OTHER PEOPLE, SEEING WHAT MAKES THEM SUCCESSFUL AND ADOPTING THOSE BEHAVIOURS YOURSELF.

Kids are experts at this. It's really quite amusing to watch Sam and Will following Jack around, mimicking everything that he does. Immensely irritating for Jack, but the others so want to be like him and do 'big boy' things. Jack only has to say something – usually 'Thunderbirds are go!' – and the other two are running around in fervid excitement shouting the same for the next 10 minutes. It's a built-in, instinctive capacity that children have for learning from others. As they grow older, the more role models they can have and identify with, the better. Relating to older children or young adults whom they like and want to be like is an important aspect of their development, aiding their passage into the big, wide world. It's an instinct that you shouldn't drop just because you've arrived in the workplace.

Don't Be Afraid of Better People

'The best executive is the one who has the sense enough to
pick good men to do what he wants done, and self-restraint
to keep from meddling with them while they do it.'

Theodore (Teddy) Roosevelt, 26th President of the USA

I will always remember arriving in Bangkok at the start of a
backpacking journey round Southeast Asia. I was fresh out of
university and had flown out to Thailand, on my own, to spend
three months travelling around Thailand, Malaysia and Indonesia
before heading off to Nepal to spend five more months doing some
voluntary work. At the time, this was all pretty big stuff for me.
These days, if I had three months ahead of me on my own, in a hot
country with nothing in particular to do, it would be absolute,
unadulterated bliss. Then, however, it was a bit on the scary side. I
had never been to a non-Western country before and here I was all
on my tod, in the middle of Bangkok. Exciting but scary. I had a
rough route planned out to fill the following weeks and headed for
the backpacking centre of Bangkok – the Kao San road.

The Kao San road is a small, bustling area crammed with hostels,
restaurants, bars and shops selling cheap, counterfeit goods. It is a
real crossroads of the world as hundreds of like-minded
backpackers mill around, en route to their next destination. It's a
very friendly place and I soon met other people heading in the
same direction, so I was not on my own for very long.

On my second night in the country, though, while sampling the
local beer, I got chatting to a guy who had just returned from Laos.
He enthusiastically extolled the virtues of Laos and how I had to
go there because everywhere else was boring and had 'been done'
before. Laos, he told me, was still relatively unexplored and
unspoiled by backpackers. I had not been out of the UK for more

than 48 hours, doing stuff that, quite frankly, was about as brave and exciting as I could manage, and here I was, being told that I was being a bit boring and mainstream. Thanks.

At that point, I learned that, no matter what you do or what you achieve, there will always be people who have done something a bit better or achieved a bit more. There will always be people 'better' than you.

The results of this from a management perspective are twofold. First, you should be secure in yourself and your own achievements in themselves and not judge yourself in relation to others. More easily said than done for some people, especially if you are very competitive, but an important thing to aspire to. Secondly, you need to recognise that being a manager does not mean being the best at everything. Far from it. There will be people in your team who are better than you at some things. In fact, if there are not, then you are probably in trouble.

> BEING A MANAGER
> DOESN'T MEAN
> BEING THE BEST
> AT EVERYTHING.
> FAR FROM IT.

Good managers actively seek out the very best people to be in their team. Their performance is dependent upon their team's performance, so they want the best people they can get. If you are insecure about not wanting to be outshone by somebody you are managing, you may be the 'best' in the office, but you won't have the best-performing team.

Recently, I watched a TV programme that compared the sexes and how men and women differed. One part was looking at how competitive men are compared with women. It showed one of the men at home with his son, playing draughts. The father explained how he couldn't possibly let the boy win – that wouldn't be 'right'. Instead, he made sure that he beat him every time. His son was six! He actually made his son cry, so upset was the boy at not winning. The dad explained that this didn't bother him because winning was more important.

This is an extreme example (or maybe not), but I think there is a bit of that in all parents, especially fathers. It's a humbling moment when the parent/teacher/mentor is overtaken by the child. Some of us accept it gracefully. Others, like the psychopath in the TV programme, are less 'adult' about it. Egos get in the way. If you take this approach when building and managing your team, however, don't be surprised when the team's performance isn't as good as you want it to be.

Network

'No man is a failure who has friends.'

Clarence, *It's a Wonderful Life* (1946)

ONE of the things that constantly amazes me about mothers is their ability to network. Where we live, the mothers' mafia is alive and strong, believe me. They say that children and dogs are the best social icebreakers. I can't vouch for dogs, but I can safely say that the theory is totally sound from a children perspective. I completely lose track of who is whose mother, which class such and such is in at school, whose husband works where, which mother is friendly with which other mother, whose father is friendly with whose mother (actually, I usually remember that bit!), which mother runs which toddler group, and so on and so forth. The whole thing makes *EastEnders* look quite simple and boring.

Now, to the untrained eye, all this looks quite quaint and lovely. Lots of women providing each other with pleasant and polite company and the odd cup of tea. Oh, no. These are crack professionals, highly skilled in the art of networking, reaching levels unimaginable to the average man. Social niceties don't come into it. Rather, an endless supply of childminders are on tap. If something's not right at school a quick phone call soon sorts out the problem, an endless supply of little playmates is available to keep the toddlers occupied while the latest brand of coffee is tested out, babysitters are never an issue, medical advice is only a phone call away and children's clothes are never in short supply. To name but a few.

If, as a manager, you can build up such a strong network, you will be onto a good thing, believe me. OK, sourcing children's clothes may not be such an issue at work, but building up a network of peers and colleagues has many advantages too. You get to hear what's really going on around the business, which is always more important than the formally reported stuff. You get to know who is moving to what position and which positions are becoming available. If you've got a difficult problem you need to sort out, you've got a pool of people you can bounce ideas off. When you need to fill a space in your team you've got people to go to for suggestions of appropriate candidates to fill the vacancy. You get to hear what's going on in other parts of the business that you wouldn't ordinarily get to hear about. The list goes on.

Building your personal network takes time and effort. But the benefits are mutual and it is perfectly possible to have a friendly, social interaction with your peers as well as reap some benefits from a business perspective.

A Tidy Desk Means a Tidy Mind!

'I'm a tidy sort of bloke. I don't like chaos. I kept records in the record rack, tea in the tea caddy, and pot in the pot box.'

George Harrison

EVERY evening (and I mean every evening) when I get home from work, I am greeted by a scene of devastation that only people who have experienced an earthquake while in Toys R Us can have been exposed to. A mass of toys, discarded shoes, half-done jigsaws, discarded clothes, books and partially eaten food litters my path from the front door to the dinner table. The obstacles a man has to overcome to get to his tea!

Now call me stupid, but every night, after the children are all tucked up in bed, I spend 15 minutes clearing this mess up in an attempt to return the house to some sort of level of normality and hygiene that is considered acceptable in modern twenty-first-century living. You can call me stupid for two reasons. First, because I should get the kids to tidy up their own mess. And you would be absolutely right. You can also call me stupid because I can absolutely guarantee that, no matter how tidy I get the house, when I get home the following evening it will be in exactly the same state of chaos.

The reason I do so, though, is simple. I just can't operate in mess. It makes me nervous! I do need things to be in a state of reasonable order so that I can get on with other things. It may be a completely unconnected activity, but if I know that something elsewhere is not sorted out, I just can't concentrate. I may want to spend the evening in front of the TV, but if I know the rest of the house is covered in toys I just can't relax.

Now I recognise that people are different and operate in different ways, and I recognise that I may be doing my reputation as a man of danger and mystery some harm here, but I am constantly amazed at the mess that some people operate within when in the office. Papers are scattered all over their desk, a cup of coffee balances on the PC, lever-arch files are piled beside and underneath the desk, Post-it notes are stuck on every available piece of spare surface, an in-tray is doing a very good impression of the Leaning Tower of Pisa, pens are scattered everywhere.

Now I'm not saying that you need to keep your workplace impeccably tidy without a thing out of place. I once worked for a manager who was keen on Japanese management fads and operated a 'clear-desk policy', which meant that everything had to be filed somewhere and your desk had to be empty of everything bar the PC and the phone at the end of each day. A real pain. I do think, however, that there needs to be some sort of order about where you work, at least at the beginning and end of each day.

Everybody generates a degree of mess while working, but papers and such should have a place where they are stored and there should be some sort of system to everything. Otherwise, your ability to think clearly about the task at hand is impaired.

We are constantly on at our kids to tidy their rooms, so it's only fair that we should be constantly on at ourselves to keep things tidy at work.

Stay in Control

> 'My father was frightened of his father. I was frightened of
> my father and I am damned well going to see to it that my
> children are frightened of me.'

King George V

MANAGEMENT is a surprisingly emotional game. Before I
entered the big, wide world of work, I always had this, admittedly
naïve, image that management was a very scientific and factual
discipline, carried out in an almost robotic way to make a
company run efficiently and smoothly. Of course, as I've learned,
and as I've shown throughout this book, this couldn't be further
from the truth.

Managers deal with human beings (usually) and human beings
have feelings and emotions. Unfortunately, these don't get
switched off when people enter the workplace. If anything, I
reckon they get turned up a few notches. As a result, it can be very
easy to get thoroughly wound up by other people. Some people do
it on purpose, to test you and your boundaries. Others are just
irritating. Learning how to recognise and control your own
emotions is therefore very important if you are to maintain your
managerial dignity. Some people can do this very easily. For others
it's much harder.

In *The Way to Win*, Will Carling and Robert Heller describe how
the former England international striker Gary Lineker approached
anger.

> *Never sent off, never even booked for any offence on the field,*
> *Lineker simply saw no point in reacting to fouls or attacking*
> *his attacker. How would that help? Fierce reaction, lashing out*
> *at the player who fouled you, didn't serve your purpose in*

playing. On the contrary, it ruined your concentration. Forcing a free kick, on the other hand, was doing your job, creating an opportunity for the team. Lineker's best policy was to get off the floor and move to a position where he might capitalise on the opening.

Many people would see such constraint as unnatural. How can you not react angrily when some dangerous, illegal footballing thug cracks your legs from beneath you? Wouldn't you have to be some emotionless, unflappable robot to keep calm? Not according to the American psychologist Dr Wayne W. Dyer. He maintains that anger is a choice which you don't have to make – and shouldn't. 'Anger gets in the way. It is good for nothing ... anger is a means of using things outside yourself to explain how you feel.'

When you're disciplining children, the choice not to get angry can be a difficult one. It's important that they know how what they have done has made you feel, but it is far more effective to tell them straight that they have made you sad, unhappy or disappointed. This way they still get the message, but you stay in control.

And there's no reason why you can't take the same approach as a manager. If something is not going well, somebody in your team has done something really stupid, or somebody is really winding you up, it is far more effective to explain to them, in a controlled manner, how they have made you feel than to let your emotions get on top of you and go off on some tirade about people's incompetence. Not only does it mean you may be able to salvage some sort of positive outcome from the situation, but you will also earn far more respect from your team. Dealing with these situations in a firm and controlled manner is far more impressive than dealing with them in an irrational and emotional manner.

Get Feedback

'Criticism is something we can avoid easily by saying nothing, doing nothing and being nothing.'

Aristotle

ONE of the signs of confident managers is that they can take criticism. In fact, they actively look for feedback on their performance, look for weaknesses, and work out ways to improve them. I've already discussed how it's important to give your team feedback on their performance. Well, you need to make sure that people do the same for you. Not just from your own boss, but from peers, your team, your customers. The more the better. This shouldn't be just a once-a-year activity for your annual appraisal, but should be constant. Go and ask them.

It's funny how, as children, we always got plenty of feedback on our performance: 'Johnny, you really need to keep your bedroom tidier; you need to be more polite to your grandmother; you played really well in the football match; why don't you make more time to finish your homework; that picture you've drawn is really good; can't you put some smarter clothes on?' And so it goes on. For some reason, in the workplace, now we're grown up, we're supposed to guess how we're doing. Quite often, as well, what we think we're good at and what we think we're bad at are not the same as other people think.

Getting good, honest feedback can be quite difficult, I accept. It can be through a subtle question in a conversation or a formal '360-degree feedback' form that you ask people to fill in, whichever is the more appropriate. The important thing is to encourage people to be as candid as possible and then to act on it.

Don't Stop Learning

'Live like you're going to die tomorrow, learn like you are going to live for ever.'

Anonymous

JUST because you've now arrived in the world of management, it doesn't mean you should stop learning. There are plenty of managers around who seem to think that, just because they have become a 'captain of industry', they must know it all and have no further need of learning. This is a huge mistake to make. Learning should be a continuous process and not something confined to schoolchildren that we suddenly stop doing once we've passed all our exams and got our first job. No matter how senior you are in an organisation, there is always something new to learn, something that many are reluctant to acknowledge for fear of showing up their weaknesses to the people who work for them.

A lot of people make the mistake of thinking that learning or development means that they have to sit in a classroom or lecture theatre being talked at by somebody with a piece of chalk in their hand. This is not the case. There are many ways to keep on learning, many of which mean you don't have to go anywhere near a classroom. In addition to the use of mentors and role models, other methods include reading books and magazine articles, talking things over with your peers and surfing the Net. Some of the best learning, though, comes from the real world and facing up to problems and challenges that confront us day in day out. By pushing yourself into situations where you face these challenges, you will learn more than you will in any classroom.

Since having children, I've been amazed at how much and how quickly they are able to learn. Their minds really are like sponges – grasping new concepts and ideas daily and remembering the most obscure facts (Daddy, remember you said last year that I could have a new Power Ranger when it was my birthday?). Watching a six-year-old pick up the intricacies of a new computer game, before his father has barely had time to start reading the instructions, is really quite alarming. Children are constantly facing new challenges – learning to walk, learning to talk, learning to read, learning to write, learning to swim, learning to do algebra, learning to speak French, learning to drive a car, and so on. As a parent, it's sometimes incomprehensible how they are going to learn the next skill expected of them; but they do. We shouldn't, therefore, let this innate ability we all have as a child disappear just because we've arrived at work.

You Get Out What You Put In

'When it comes to getting jobs done, it is hard work that really counts.'

The Fat Controller, *Thomas the Tank Engine*

A couple of years ago, Melanie and I decided that it would be a good thing to start to take the boys camping. A wholesome, healthy pursuit to teach them the beauty and joy of the great outdoors – and several years' worth of cheap holidays to boot! It seemed like a great idea. The only drawback was the lack of hair drying facilities – for Melanie that is, not me. Inconvenient, but not insurmountable.

Having purchased an Outwell Hartford XL tent (East Wing and West Wing included), we organised our first weekend away – with some friends, just in case things got too difficult. Destination: Buttyland campsite near Tenby! We set off in high spirits, with a car full of spanking-new camping equipment, looking forward to losing our camping virginity, so to speak. As we got to the other side of the Severn Bridge, however, the traffic on the M4 came to a grinding halt.

Not to worry, we thought. Once we're passed Cardiff, it'll free up. But oh, no. Three hours later we were still crawling along at no more that 30 mph, wondering why we were still east of Swansea and not sitting outside our Outwell Hartford XL drinking mugs of steaming tea and taking in deep breaths of fresh air! Half an hour later, just to cheer us up, a thumping black cloud appeared and it started to rain. Great!

At this point, Will, quite understandably, decided that three and a half hours strapped in a car seat, being amused by nothing more than his father attempting to pronounce Welsh names on motorway signs, in a vaguely comedic Welsh accent, was unreasonable. He began to wail. Not a minor, slightly irritated cry, but a full-blown, bloodcurdling fit of screaming. After trying every trick in the book to calm him down, and failing miserably, we stopped the car in the next lay-by for a time-out – in the rain. Quite frankly, it was all looking a bit grim.

Neither Melanie nor I said anything, but we knew the same thing was going through both our minds. What on earth were we doing (to put it politely)? We had gone too far to turn back for home and the kids could take little, if any, more driving anyway. The traffic was rubbish and the black cloud was extending far into the distance. Suddenly, the hairdryer issue seemed a minor one.

> IT'S THE DIFFICULT SITUATIONS THAT YOU REALLY LEARN FROM, NOT THE EASY ONES.

Anyway, we carried on and eventually, after four and a half hours, arrived at Buttyland – only to find that the fish-and-chip van we had planned to get tea from (this isn't the Boy Scouts, you know) had a sign outside saying that it didn't open until the following weekend! Fortunately, though, the rain had stopped, so we got on with putting up the tent as quickly as possible before it started again.

And after that things steadily improved. The tent went up a treat (even if I say so myself). Our friends sourced some excellent fish and chips from an alternative supplier. The kids ran around having a whale of a time and slept through the night like logs. The following day was even sunny and we had a great time visiting a castle, having a pub lunch and playing on the beautiful, sandy beach. We even got to drink the mugs of steaming tea outside the tent in the evening. At the end of the weekend, as we drove home in the sun, with the kids fast asleep in the back of the car, we both agreed that we had all had an excellent time and that when we got home we would get straight on with sorting out the next trip.

The point of all this, other than to recommend camping at Buttyland, is that I do believe that sometimes you have to 'go through it' to achieve the really worthwhile things – both at home and at work. It's the difficult situations that you really learn from and that you can take something away from, not the easy ones.

I've been there myself – I had no idea how I was going to deliver a project, was struggling with difficult team members, lost lots of sleep over it, would wake up in the night in cold sweats, dreaded going into work, couldn't stop thinking about work at the weekends and was convinced that I was going to be sacked. It was not a pleasant time. However, I came through and did deliver. I know that I learned more in those six months than at any other time. It also raised my confidence levels markedly. Knowing that I could cope with the stress and could come up with the goods was invaluable and has meant that I have been able to tackle similar, if not, tougher, situations since with a conviction that I would not have had without going through the experience.

There are plenty of people around who make a career out of avoiding things that look difficult and looking for the easy life. Believe me, it would be far easier to sit the kids in front of the TV all weekend than take them camping to some bizarrely named campsite in South Wales. But if you want to develop yourself as a manager who stands out above the rest, then you need to be prepared to put yourself into difficult situations from time to time and test yourself.

One of my heroes is Leonardo Da Vinci. He was an amazing man who pushed himself and the boundaries of science, medicine, engineering and art. Apparently, he was asked on his deathbed whether he was scared of dying. His response was that he felt quite the contrary – very relaxed, as he would at the end of a hard day's work. We can avoid the difficult things, but, when I'm on my deathbed, I intend to feel the same way as Da Vinci.

Commitment and Persistence

'Champions keep playing until they get it right.'

Billy Jean King, retired US tennis player

I always remember when some friends came to lunch in those quiet, calm, lazy days before we had children. Our friends, on the other hand, brought their two young boys. We didn't really know anybody else with children at the time, so the normal preparations were made involving, among other things, salad with exotic dressing and a carefully chosen red wine. Since we hadn't seen our friends for a while, we were looking forward to a couple of hours of sophisticated conversation and good food.

However, from the minute our friends walked through the door to the time they left later that afternoon, our humble home experienced chaos and pandemonium on a scale that Melanie and I had just never seen before. While we were all supposed to be enjoying aperitifs, the children walked and crawled around the house looking for the most interesting ornaments to play with. During most of the meal, the mother was standing up next to the younger boy in his high chair, desperately trying to time her lunges with a spoonful of goo with his opening his mouth at random intervals.

At the same time, her husband tried to convince their elder child that crying his eyes out and screaming because he didn't like tomatoes was unacceptable. Most of the dessert had to be scraped up off the floor. It seemed pointless even bothering to offer anybody wine – nobody would have heard me anyway.

After they had all left, Melanie and I collapsed onto the sofa, physically and mentally exhausted. We didn't have any energy left to say anything, but we both looked at each other thinking the same thing: how on earth do you cope with that every day, day in, day out?

And yet here we are, a few years later, with three of our own, coping day in, day out. Sometimes, we even enjoy it! Yes, it's hard work; yes, there are days when you are willing bedtime to arrive; and, yes, we're now the ones who go to other people's houses and see the look of panic as Will toddles about clutching their best bone china. But we wouldn't miss it for the world. That's how you feel when you're committed to something and are prepared to be persistent in the effort that's necessary to make it work.

Commitment is important for managers, too. If you're not committed to what you turn up to work for, day in, day out, then you're not going to be motivated and you're not going to perform. If you're going to be a successful manager, therefore, it really does help if you are working on something, or for somebody, you feel committed to.

I have to admit, there have been times in my career when I have I found it difficult to feel 100 per cent committed to what I'm doing. That has never been the case while I've been at Airbus, though. I don't know why I like aeroplanes. At the end of the day, I suppose it's a boyish fascination with big toys! On a day-to-day basis, there are still occasions now when I find what I'm doing mundane or uninspiring. However, my overall feeling of commitment is different because I can relate to the end product and what it does. In the way that commitment to your family and children helps you put up with some of the less glamorous jobs, such as changing nappies, commitment to your work helps you go through some of the day-to-day grind that everybody has to face, no matter how great their job. If you are totally committed to and really want to achieve the end result, you will.

In addition, achieving results requires persistence. Things rarely come good first time.

Some of the highest achievers in history have been people who have persisted – often against the odds. Edison, who produced thousands of light bulbs before inventing one that worked, said, 'Genius is one per cent inspiration and 99 per cent perspiration.' Anybody who has watched a baby learning to stand will know how important persistence is from an early age. It's a habit that no manager should forget.

Dream

'Daddy, what do you want to be when you grow up?'

Sam Durston

WHEN Sam asked me the question above, I laughed (though not as much as Melanie did!). Then I actually thought that maybe it wasn't such a ridiculous question after all. It's so easy to get carried away with the day-to-day, and bogged down in the detail of the numerous challenges we face, that we lose sight of the bigger picture. Taking time to stand back and think about where we're going, not tomorrow, or next week, but in two, five, ten years' time, is something that few of us find time for. As children we dream about the job we want to do when we're adults. Maybe we should keep on making a point of asking ourselves what we want to be when we grow up?

Afterword

It's Like Riding a Bike

'A leader is best when people barely know he exists. Not so good when people obey and acclaim him. Worse when they despise him. But of a good leader who talks little, when his work is done and his aim fulfilled, they will say, "We did it ourselves".'

Jack Smith, former CEO of General Motors

I haven't written this book because I think it will solve all the management problems of the world. It's much better to see it as another brick in the wall of your own development. As I've already said, don't stop learning. When you do, you're in trouble. Keep putting that school blazer on every now and then and get yourself on a course, read journals, surf the Net, do a job you've not done before, read another book. I would highly recommend reading some of those listed at the back of this one. They're not just there to fill another page. There's so much good stuff out there – explore it. Be curious.

Some things will work for you, others won't. Try things. Test them. Play around with them. Push them as hard as you can. Do what kids do and see whether you can break them. If you can't and they work for you, great, use them. If the wheels come off, discard them and try something else. It's a continuous process. You don't one day become a qualified manager and that's it. It's something you can improve right up until the day you get given the carriage clock and go home to spend more time in the garden.

Managers are often asked to summarise detailed reports or complex situations with a 'one-pager' (this is the twenty-first century and everybody, after all, is very busy). Well, for mine, I'll leave you with one last thing I learned from my kids.

Many fathers (and a few mothers) have spent an afternoon in the park or in the road outside their house, running behind their child who is learning to ride his (or her) bike. The stabilisers have been removed and lucky Dad gets to run up and down like a complete idiot, clutching the back of the saddle. Slowly turning redder and redder, he regrets the missed sessions at the local gym he joined at Christmas – and the curry the night before.

He's had to convince his child that he's now far too old to be using stabilisers and that cycling without them, while more difficult at first, will be much more fun in the long run. 'If you can learn to ride by Christmas, maybe Santa will bring you a new, big bike,' says Dad.

He has had to spend time showing the child how to start off with one foot on the ground and how to feel the balance of the bike. The child has to trust Dad to keep him upright while he gets used to two wheels instead of four. No doubt there are times when everything goes at bit wobbly and the child comes off – hopefully with nothing more than a grazed knee. Dad has to convince them that it's OK to get back on and try again. When the child says he's had enough and he wants to have his stabilisers back, Dad has to insist that it's worth carrying on trying. When the child eventually starts to get going and builds up some momentum Dad shouts, 'That's it, you're getting the hang of it.'

Over a period of time the child slowly gets better and better, and gradually, almost imperceptibly, confidence increases.

Then one day, Dad makes a brave decision. The child is careering along at speed, concentrating hard, looking forward intently.

Slowly, Dad lets go.

Bibliography

Amos, Julie-Ann, 2002, *You're in Charge Now*, Oxford: How To Books.

Badaracco Jr, Joseph L., and Ellsworth, Richard R., 1989, *Leadership and the Quest for Integrity*, Boston: Harvard Business School Press.

Belbin, R. Meredith, 1981, *Management Teams – Why They Succeed or Fail*, London: Butterworth-Heinemann.

Biddulph, Steve, 1998, *Raising Boys*, London: Thorsons.

Biddulph, Steve, 1998, *The Secret of Happy Children*, London: Thorsons.

Blanchard, Kenneth, and Johnson, Spencer, 1996, *The One Minute Manager*, London: HarperCollins Business.

Carling, Will, and Heller, Robert, 1995, *The Way to Win*, London: Little, Brown.

Davidson, Jeff, 1997, *The Complete Idiot's Guide to Assertiveness*, Indianapolis: Alpha Books.

Ford, Gina, 2000, *From Contented Baby to Confident Child*, London: Vermilion.

Gallwey, Timothy, 2003, *The Inner Game of Work*, New York: Texere.

BIBLIOGRAPHY

George, Bill, 2003, *Authentic Leadership*, San Francisco: Jossey-Bass.

Green, Christopher, 2001, *New Toddler Taming*, London: Vermilion.

James, Oliver, 2003, *They F*** You Up*, London: Bloomsbury.

Johnson, Spencer, 1999, *Who Moved My Cheese?*, London: Vermilion.

McDermott, Steve, 2002, *How To Be a Complete and Utter Failure in Life, Work and Everything*, Harlow: Prentice Hall Business.

Parker, Jan, and Stimpson, Jan, 1999, *Raising Happy Children*, London: Hodder & Stoughton.

Parsons, Rob, 1995, *The Sixty Minute Father*, London: Hodder & Stoughton.

Parsons, Rob, and Parsons, Lloyd, 1999, *What Every Kid Wished Their Parents Knew ... and vice versa*, London: Hodder & Stoughton.

Robbins, Stephen P., 2003, *The Truth About Managing People*, New Jersey: Prentice Hall.

Thomas, Elwyn, and Woods, Mike, 1992, *The Manager's Casebook*, London: Michael Joseph.

Tuckmann, Bruce C., 1965, 'Development Sequences in Small Groups', *Psychological Bulletin*, vol. 3, no. 6.

Acknowledgements

APART from the three young stars who feature throughout, this book would not have been possible without two people.

First, my wife, Melanie. I am indebted to her for all her hard work and support during its writing, and especially for her dogged reading through the numerous drafts when I know she would have rather been reading *Harry Potter*.

Also, Albert DePetrillo of Piatkus. Thank you for being able to see the 'wood' this book has become among the trees of my first draft.

Finally, thank you to everybody I have had the pleasure of working with over the years. To learn what constitutes good management, I have simply watched you guys and remembered the good bits.

All mistakes are mine.

Permissions

Amos, Julie-Ann, *You're in Charge Now*, How To Books, 2002
Reprinted by kind permission of How To Books Ltd.

Badaracco Jr, Joseph L. & Ellsworth, Richard R., *Leadership and the Quest for Integrity*, Harvard Business School Press, 1993
Extract reprinted by permission of Harvard Business School Publishing

Biddulph, Steve, *Raising Boys*, HarperCollins, 1998
Extract reprinted in the UK and Europe by permission of HarperCollins Publishers Ltd., (Steve Biddulph) (1998)

Biddulph, Steve, *Raising Boys*, Finch, 2003
Extract reprinted in the Rest of the World by permission of Finch Publishers

Biddulph, Steve, *The Secret of Happy Children*, HarperCollins, 1999
Extract reprinted by permission of HarperCollins Publishers Ltd., (Steve Biddulph) (1999)

Carling, Will and Heller, Robert, *The Way to Win*, Little, Brown, 1995
Extract reprinted by permission of Little, Brown

Green, Dr Christopher, *New Toddler Taming*, Vermilion (Random House), 2005
Extract reprinted by permission of The Random House Group Ltd.

PERMISSIONS

McDermott, Steve, *How to be a Complete and Utter Failure*, Pearson Education, 2002
Extract reprinted by permission of Pearson Education

Parker, Jan & Stimpson, Jan, *Raising Happy Children*, Hodder and Stougton, 1999
Extract reprinted by permission of Hodder and Stoughton Ltd.

Parsons, Rob, *The Sixty Minute Father*, Hodder and Stoughton, 1995
Extract reprinted by permission of Hodder and Stoughton Ltd.

Robbins, Stephen P., *The Truth About Managing People*, Pearson Education, 2003
Extract reprinted by permission of Pearson Education

Szita, Jane, 'I Play, Therefore I Am', KLM in-flight magazine, July 2004